FREAKS & FIRE

FREAKS & FIRE
THE UNDERGROUND REINVENTION OF CIRCUS

BY
J. DEE HILL

PHOTOGRAPHY BY
PHIL HOLLENBECK

SOFT SKULL PRESS

Freaks and Fire: The Underground Reinvention of Circus
ISBN: 1-932360-52-2

Cover design by Joel Tippie
Cover art by Jeff Barfoot

Published by Soft Skull Press
71 Bond Street, Brooklyn, NY 11217

Distributed by Publishers Group West
www.pgw.com 1.800.788.3123

Printed in Hong Kong

Library of Congress Cataloging-in-Publication Data

Hill, Dee J.
Freaks and fire / Dee J. Hill.
p. cm.
ISBN 1-932360-52-2 (alk. paper)
1. Circus. 2. Circus performers. I. Title.
GV1815.H55 2004
791. 3—dc22

2004013836

CONTENTS

TO ALL THE FREAKS

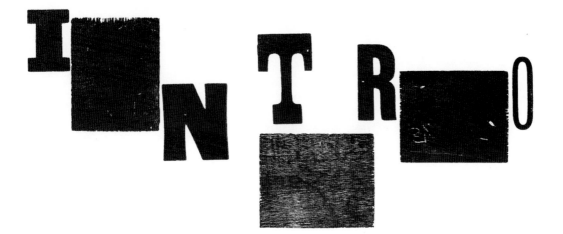

INTRODUCTION

I WALKED INTO a diner in south Austin one hot Sunday afternoon to meet an acquaintance I knew from the Burning Man festival. My friend Brett—a philosopher also known as DJ Princess Death Bunny—was already waiting there, the glass of water in front of him piled high with ice and sweating in the sultry Texas heat. He was beaming and obviously happy to see me.

"Hey I want you to meet one of my friends," he called to the waitress as I sat down. The heavily tattooed, pierced and pink-haired girl walked over, looking a bit uncertain. "Meet Dee," Brett said. He added in approving tones, "She's one of us. She's a freak."

A freak. I'm not sure at what point that became a term of approbation, but there it was. I had been kissed with the freak seal of approval and something in me glowed Possibly because I don't look anything like a freak—no tattoos, no special appendages, I even stopped wearing pierced earrings years ago. It made the bestowal of the name even better: I had been acknowledged for my inner freak.

I kept thinking about that introduction long after we ate lunch, paid the bill and left the restaurant Freak has come to mean something slightly different than its original definition. Freak implies both a larger community in which the individual is shunned, or at least regarded with vague suspicions, for his or her peculiarities, and a smaller community in which those peculiarities are embraced. It's about relationships, not just physical anomalies.

To the extent that all individuals, at one time or another, feel they are misunderstood, alienated, or just have something weird growing on their bodies (What is that lump on your neck? The beginnings of a second head?), everyone carries within them a sort of latent freak. That is, freak has its place; it's a part of human nature and not just the lot of a sad few. But in what location or context does the inner freak find expression?

THE GATHERING OF TRIBES

An ancient caravan creaks into view, wooden wheels turning, a mixture of animal smells and tinkling bells all washed in a mysterious rosy light that is ever cast over the horizon by the dawn of civilization. This is the place. Or rather, the non-place, for as we see, this rolling compound of people/animals/babies/tools is nomadic, and it stops only to trade. This string of wagons is the ancient, archetypal tribe.

Anthropologists plot this image early in the timeline of the development of human civilization, early in the trajectory that leads from blood-related family units, to tribal villages, to nation-states, and finally, only recently, to the global economy. The place of the freak is with the tribe, a level of social integration that is larger than the family but small enough that the individual's personal peculiarities or proclivities determine their inclusion.

This level of tribal affiliation, and the experience of community it provides, is problematic in the modern world. Traditional forms of the tribe, like the village, have almost completely disappeared. Fewer and fewer people live in small communities where their daily interactions bring them in contact with the people they are deeply connected to, either spiritually or economically. Workers in modern corporations are replaceable and no longer bound to each other by the experience of a shared interdependence. The modern individual is preoccupied simultaneously by the isolating, immediate concerns of personal survival and the larger, often intangible concerns of war, terror and economic change as transmitted by a now-seamless global media network. The intermediate space of community is not easily reached.

Not by accident, many of the newer, emergent forms of culture include a specifically tribal aspect. A return to tattooing, scarification, fire performance and drumming, as well as a renewed interest in ritual, has occurred side-by-side with the formation of intentional (if temporary) communities such as the Rainbow Family gatherings and Burning Man festival, all of which focus on celebrating and integrating the peculiarities of their varied members.

It was at these kinds of festivals, in clubs and at underground raves, that alternative circus acts began appearing in the early 90s. The performers were young, crazy "freaks" without any formal training who used circus costumes, skills or themes as a performative means for expressing their own exaggerated personalities. Many went on to gain formal training or to study the history of the genre. But essentially their relationship to conventional circuses resembled that of outsider art to mainstream art circles. They didn't really relate to the modern-day circus. They took their cues from something much, much older: the caravan-pulling gypsies.

The gypsies, shunned by society at large, but fiercely loyal to their own clan, were the most tribal group of all in Europe. It was these wanderers who first produced circus-like entertainments in medieval townships, along with strolling players and minstrel shows. It wasn't until the 1770s that Englishman Philip Astley fused military equestrian drills with acrobatics and other entertainments to form the modern circus.

The phenomenon of alternative circus performance can be seen as the theatrical dimension to one generation's wholesale rediscovery of the concept of the tribe. Their position is reminiscent of the strolling players in Ingmar Bergman's *The Seventh Seal*. In the film, the traveling circus performers, with their innocence and play, are the only survivors of the plague, represented as a sort of disease of the human spirit incarnate in the Crusades. Circus, the tribal entertainment, eludes the modern world with its malaises and plagues.

This is not mere regression or a rejection of modernity. (After all, few "modern primitives" want to be without their cell phones or Internet access.) Rather, it is an attempt to embrace the root, to continue to hold tribal affiliation as a foundation upon which more complex means of relating can be built.

Throughout his many works, systems theorist and philosopher Ken Wilber maps out a course of human social (and spiritual) development as not merely linear, but "holistic"—in the sense of fractal-like holons. Each level of development, each holon, contains and expands upon the level of development which preceded it. Contrary to the usual assumption that progress gets rid of all the inferior, outmoded forms, Wilber suggests that higher levels of development preserve the lower while suffusing them with new meaning. But there are risks.

"The fact that evolution always produces greater transcendence . . . means that a factor of *possible* pathology is built into every evolutionary step, because transcendence *can* go too far and become *repression*—the higher does not negate and preserve the lower, it tries only to negate (or repress or deny) the lower, which works about as well as denying our feet."[1]

A return to tribalism is taking place—but reinvented from the perspective of the holon which follows it: that is to say, without the ethnocentrism, without the fear of outsiders, without irrational taboos, without the many flaws which flowed from the original form of tribal affiliation. Tribes are sought that sustain the individual, in all his or her peculiarities, while preserving access to global consciousness.

We have become nomadic again, by car and by airplane; and are primitives once more in our quest for the primary things (values, relationships) that define us. The nomadic, primitive, tribal circus has re-emerged to entertain us on this journey.

CIRCUS AS SHAMANISM

Art and medicine are often one and the same at the tribal level. The healer and performer were embodied in a single character: the shaman. Circus in particular makes direct reference to the shamanic arts: the journey to the upper realms on the trapeze or the nether worlds marked by fire (led by the Ringmaster, often a sort of demonic spirit guide), dismemberment (knife-throwing), and transformation resulting in various supernatural powers—such as the ability to fly through the air with the greatest of ease.

Clowns, for example, are full of shamanic references. "The ability to take on a different persona or personae while in an altered state of consciousness is typical of the trickster or sacred clown in tribal cultures. They 'shift' shape and, at times, their antics become very extreme," comments art historian and critic Mark Levy in his book *Technicians of Ecstasy*. Referring especially to the sacred clowns of the Pueblo Indians, he continues, "In tribal societies, where a strict hierarchy of social conventions prevails, the trickster extends the boundaries of the permissible and interjects a much needed spirit of disorder."[2]

The shamanic journey was traditionally undertaken in order to bring healing to the tribe, and it was done by someone who had been set apart as "different," either because of sickness, visions or a particularly arduous initiation. Some current-day alternative circuses, composed of people "set apart," consciously make community healing a part of their work as well. This is particularly noticeable in groups that adopt mythological themes for their performances.

An Austin-based fire performer with the stage name Arashi, who is a member of the fire troupe Tantien, provides an example. "The people I am family with are mostly shamanic people who cultivate their own spirit and magic," he says.

"I don't feel separation from society. I feel like I'm trying to provide my piece of the pie. It is the job of the shaman to keep people aware of other worlds and other possibilities. It's a service to society for me. I try not to have a cosmic schism through anger or rebellion . . . I know I'm a freak and I know a lot of people may not be open to shamanic stuff (although I'm not saying I'm a shaman—that would be pretentious). But I'm all about trying to break down barriers between people.

"I'm an artistic person. I've got dreadlocks and piercings and everything coming off my body. In my younger years I was a punk rock kid and I hated authority and I still don't agree with a lot of things people in authority do. But I went through my own internal process about hate and realized it wasn't going to solve anything. I'm kind of out of that whole negative thing. When [Tantien] first started, our shows were integrated into trance dancing—outdoor dance parties out in the woods. People would come to dance and we would bust out our fire in the middle of it and make it into a communal rite. People would come up to us afterwards and say, 'This has changed our lives.'"

Rogan P. Taylor, who provides some of the most intriguing links between circus and shamanism in *The Death and Resurrection Show*, says, "The enthusiasm which the audiences showed for these archaic relics of magical consciousness seems to bear a direct relationship to the progress of modern technology. It seems that the more embroiled we became in the rationality of materialism, the more enthusiastically we sought our entertainment in the irrational worlds of magic. The more isolated we felt from the new priesthood of scientists, the more we liked the shows which encouraged direct participation. For another hallmark of these shaman-oriented performances is the readiness with which the barriers between the show and the audience are broken down."[3]

PURE PLAY: CONSUMERISM AND THE DO-IT-YOURSELF CIRCUS

"Circus is about play—the rediscovery and affirmation of play, much more than it is about skill," says a fan of Circus Contraption, a Seattle-based indie circus. "Cirque du Soleil is about skill, to a level where it almost doesn't seem human. But when Circus Contraption performs, you can almost see yourself up there."

The deliberately homemade feel of some of these troupes is endearing to some, dreadful to others.

Gypsy Snider is the consummate circus insider. She was born into a circus family (her parents, Larry Pisoni and Peggy Snider, formed San Francisco's long-running Pickle Family Circus), entertained audiences around the world herself as a performer for many years, and is now director of the regrouped New Pickle Circus. She is skeptical of the new generation of alternative circus performers.

"What tends to bother me about people going, 'Oh, let's make a circus' is that it is an art form and takes incredible amounts of discipline and training," she says. "All too often people kind of take it lightly. They say, 'Oh, isn't it fun?' It is not fun. It is incredibly brutal on the body and the heart. In terms of small circus companies, I've seen a few that have completely offended me and some that have blown my socks off."

Take the Bindlestiff Family Cirkus,[4] for example. "I saw them once—it was raw, like a medicine/freakshow, which I actually loved as a concept," she says. "Unfortunately I felt it was really lacking in substance and missing a theatrical quality. It was like, 'what we're doing is so vulgar and out there that you're gonna love it.' I love to see ugly things because I believe a true beauty lies in ugliness, but you have to do more than throw that at the audience. There's an artistry behind the delivery that's important. I felt they just thought they were so cool they didn't have to master that artistry." But she goes on to add, "There's something beautiful in circus, in that you go into a different world and that's what was nice about Bindlestiff—we did go into their world, into this dirty kind of forbidden circus peep show."

For many of these new players, the level of artistry isn't the point. The point, much like punk rock, it that *they* are the ones doing it. They are making their own fun, creating their own entertainment rather than consuming it, and infecting the audience with a sense of possibility and participation. An anti-consumer ethic pervades the underground circus, along with performance styles that bring audience members onstage or even break down the performer/spectator barrier altogether. We see ourselves in their performances and cheer that much harder for the clown struggling to juggle another ball. And if the ball drops or the tightrope walker slips—so what? We're all tripping fools in ridiculous costumes anyway.

This sense of identification is closely related to the effectiveness of the circus experience as shamanistic ritual. Ritual, as opposed to entertainment, is effective to the extent that the audience believes that what is happening on stage is also happening to them. For the performers of the underground circus, the show is not about acting, it's about being who they really are—freaks—and uncovering for all the world to see their most mad, strange, divine selves.

— J. Dee Hill

NOTES

1. Ken Wilber, The Collected Works of Ken Wilber, vol. 6: Sex, Ecology, Spirituality: The Spirit of Evolution, 2d ed., rev. (Boston & London, Shambhala, 2000), pp. 107-8.

2. Mark Levy, Technicians of Ecstacy: Shamanism and the Modern Artist (Norforld, Conn.: Bramble Books, 1993), p. 262-3.

3. Rogan P. Taylor, The Death and Resurrection Show: From Shaman to Superstar (Century Hutchinson, 1985), p.131.

4. Bindlestiff Family Cirkus, see Chapter 8.

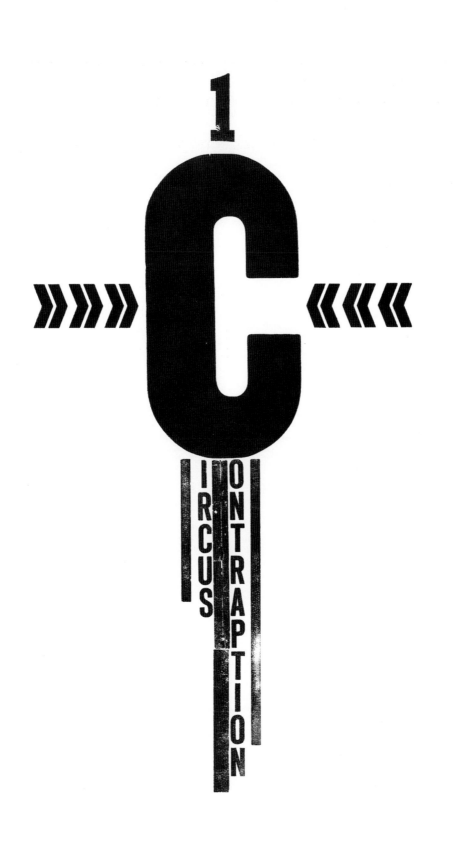

A SPOTLIGHT CASTS its greenish hue on the enigmatic figure of Dr. Calamari, a strange gentleman in a bowler hat astride a fantastical vehicle, equal parts bicycle, wagon and Tim Burton-inspired nightmare. A creaking accordion accompanies his progress and the turning of the strange engine's wheels.

"Hello Acrophelia," he calls in a merry voice that sends a chill of suspicion through the audience "I'm off to give the aardvarks their weekly dose of ketamine!" A syringe drops casually to the ground.

Little Acrophelia, a girl with enormous eyes recalling morose drawings of Victorian children, grabs the fallen syringe, accidentally impales herself and dies. Dr. Calamari discovers that his wagon conveniently converts to a coffin-shaped hearse.

The end.

The horrified audience can't help but laugh at this bit of black humor. A few acts later, Acrophelia returns as a life-size puppet, imploring her lover Dr. Calamari to take his own life and join her in the ground. Then the real Acrophelia rises from her coffin to perform an acrobalancing act with Dr. Calamari (or as they call it, "necrobalancing")—a series of slow gymnastic poses in which the partners balance and hold each other, often seeming to defy the laws of gravity. The two rouse the audience to cheering with their feats until Acrophelia once again falls, lifeless as a doll, into the sorrowful Calamari's arms.

It's this sort of dark vaudeville, drawn on the true experience and intimations of childhood, that reminds us of the nether side of circus—why, for example, we thought clowns were pretty scary at one point in our early lives. Add to that prescient sense of terror a few more unseemly items—sock-holes covered by spangles and sequins, melancholy converted to wanderlust, madness and gin-soaked dreams—and you have the fuel for the onstage phenomenon of Circus Contraption.

Circus Contraption began in 1998 as a collaboration between David Crellin, at that time the frontman for a band called Phineas Gage, and Lara Paxton: dancer, aerialist and visionary extraordinaire. David, whose band already had a pronounced circus theme, transformed himself into the bombastic circus barker Armitage Shanks. (The name is that of a well-known British plumbing fixture company. His friends in Europe tell him they think of him whenever they use the toilet.)

Lara had been learning the traditional aerialist skills of the rope and tissu (the name derives from the French word for "fabric") for several years following a varied career as both a stripper and midwife. Now aged thirty-four, she wears her hair in four trademark pigtails while doing breathtaking splits and contortions suspended in midair. As artistic director, she inspires much of the circus' feel and flavor with her own fantasies, which she says are influenced by dream states and the writings of psychedelic social critic Terence McKenna.

"One morning I just woke up thinking about aardvarks," she says. "I had an overwhelming desire to make these aardvark masks. Sometimes I think the whole circus began as an excuse for me to make them.

"It was a dream kind of like when you're just waking up in the morning and half asleep. I feel more lucid right then. I was awake enough to remember what I was dreaming and be like, 'oh yeah, this is a good idea.'"

In a short period of less than a month, dreams supplied Lara with all the basic materials needed for the first show. They arrived "boom-boom-boom," says Lara. "It was this whole stable of images. I felt really lucky. It was like, 'oh good, I have six little acts that I can just put together.' And that was enough for the first show, with a couple of jugglers and a few volunteer artists."

The aardvark masks became the hallmark of the first show, in which they appeared on the heads of ballerinas dancing *en pointe*. After that the bizarre mammal became something of a running joke for the group. A baby aardvark showed up in a baby carriage in "All Fall Down," a show devoted to childhood games and nightmares based on the black plague-inspired poem "Ring Around the Rosy."

Lara looks—and moves—like a little girl herself, with her quadruple pigtails decked with multicolored ribbons. She sits crosslegged on a folding chair, a froth of purple petticoats stacked behind her on a table.

"Right after I started doing trapeze, David and I were talking about how fun it would be to do a circus-based performance group. And we had originally thought that it would be a lot more conceptual, or less literally circus. We didn't think we'd have actual jugglers!" she says.

She was managing a yoga studio at the time when three jugglers looking for rehearsal space walked in the front door. They were swiftly invited to join and David began putting a new band together. "The first show . . . was pretty funky," says Lara. "We've gotten a lot more polished since then, in a good way, I think. One of the things we want to avoid is getting too overproduced and polished. We always want to feel like we're approachable."

On a cold Seattle night in early spring, the ticket line for the latest show, "Gallimaufry—An Evening of Jiggery-Pokery," runs down a hallway and outside the converted naval base where the circus has its home. The cast members are joyous. At least one person can recall a show in which only about four people came, all of them with complimentary tickets.

Tonight's show, by contrast, is in high demand. As the paying public enters, they encounter a makeshift midway, complete with popcorn vendors, sideshow banners and a boundlessly energetic one-armed juggler who tosses axes and jokes about the likely loss of another appendage.

Groupies are noticeable in the audience, as they mill along the midway. The circus has its own camp followers who come to the show in clown-white makeup and outlandish garb. Some of them take lessons from the circus once a week in gymnastics, aerial and clowning; others are just there to rub shoulders with their favorite performers. Despite the chill inside the naval base, one young man is wearing nothing but a red silk bathrobe open to the navel, accessorized by a brandy snifter full of beer, a cheroot, and a finely drawn, sleazy moustache in black grease pencil. A girl wears a leather bra and tap pants over a red fishnet bodystocking. Altogether they form a ghastly assembly of freaks who look as if they'd died, decomposed and been reanimated a few days later to fill out the cast of "Cabaret."

"We had a bigger midway last year for the first forty-five minutes of the show that I'm sort of missing," says Lara. "We had all these games that had twists on them, like 'Cock Ringer.' Colin the juggler had a big strap-on and it was like a ring toss. It was really, really funny. Another one was called 'Buy a Politician,' which was a beanbag toss. There were little dollar signs on the beanbags and you threw them into his pocket or into his mouth. I got cotton candy and strapped some racks on the sides of my stilts so people could buy cotton candy from the stilts. We had some hoochie-coochie dancers. And we had a peep show where Jason [Dr. Calamari] was just acting really weird, playing the ukulele in his underwear with a little weird mask—it was completely trippy and hilarious.

"But we also had little dramas going on. Like my character, Darty Kangoo, would be the secret admirer of Chameleo. So I would find an audience member and say, 'See that man over there—I love him! Give him this note but don't tell him who it's from!' We tried to keep this storyline going and interact with the audience, so by the time we marched in to the stage for the actual show they were on our side, you know what I mean? I still feel like they're on our side, but it's not quite the same when we're just backstage the whole time until the show starts."

* * *

Meanwhile another scene unfolds backstage, beginning with a hole in a sock. It is a miniscule hole, tiny, resting on the accordionist's ankle just a half inch above the edge of a well-worn black shoe. Its wearer, Greg Adair (a.k.a. Harold Smaude), is tragically saying, "It was nice, she left me for a tuba player," as he smears white pancake makeup over his face. He adds rouge to his lips and the tip of his nose while gazing into a profoundly filthy backstage mirror.

I am captivated by the appearance of the hole in his sock as he continues his story, mentally comparing it with his black suit, bow tie, $6 bowler hat and borrowed accordion—the shabby splendor of circus life. A musician by trade who formally studied everything from Eastern European gypsy music to flamenco, Greg traveled across the country hitchhiking and—he admits—drinking, until he met the circus. He liked the gypsy music and the gypsy lifestyle that accompanied the troupe, and quickly taught himself accordion.

Makeup finished, he places the bowler on his head, noting that one day he is going to buy himself a "real" hat. "We're all so poor," he says. "We paid ourselves $20 a week on our last tour, which barely supports my smoking habit, much less my drinking habit. I was living on drink tickets and cheap bottles of whiskey last summer." Many of the other cast members experience their own version of Greg's predicament, an eternal battle between paying rent and spending just a few more dollars on a spangled costume or a musical instrument.

For now Greg lives in the back of a converted van, occasionally sleeping on an ancient green couch in the backstage dressing room, where he can keep an eye on the group's gear.

"I'm kind of depressed," Greg confides. "Nice, healthy, rosy-cheeked girls can't stay with me; they don't like the way I treat myself. Anyway," he says, rousing himself from a melancholic slump, "I'm writing an opera right now. I couldn't possibly have a relationship, I'm so focused on my work."

Greg isn't always so dour. But sometimes it's hard to differentiate between the character he plays, the grim-natured Harold Smaude, and the accomplished musician who plays the guitar, banjo, saw, toy piano and anything else he can get his hands on. He wrote the accordion-based song "Ode to My Employer" (opening line: "I will piss on your grave when you die . . .") based on a real-life episode. "I wrote it in about two minutes on the way to quitting a temp slave-labor job that was an absolute nightmare," he states.

"I'm living in the van now in hopes of not having to pay rent and maybe survive on less. My grandparents have lived in their RV all their lives—they're full-on vagabonds—so it's maybe not a new idea to me." It means freedom, he says, "freedom from just about everything that ties people down in their lives these days—you know, some stagnant, immobile jobs and shit. I can't deal with it, I've never been good at dealing with it, which is probably why I'm here.

"I want to be a fucking gypsy. I've traveled around the country just drinking and hitchhiking but this is better. It's a way to meet people and bring something into the community. It's a means of being in this world and being comfortable in your skin. It's a way to give something—hitchhiking is just taking."

Colin Ernst, juggler and metal sculptor, enters the dressing room through the back door, talking about building a giant whirligig on stage whose movements would be triggered by falling sand.

"That would be beautiful," comments Greg. "We're Circus Contraption but we have yet to live up to the contraption end of the circus. Colin makes some cool shit like that coffin-wagon thing. We're all into things like Rube Goldberg contraptions but we have yet to make a show based on those themes." He traces red lipgloss over his mouth, then grimaces to check the effect of his wetly shining lips.

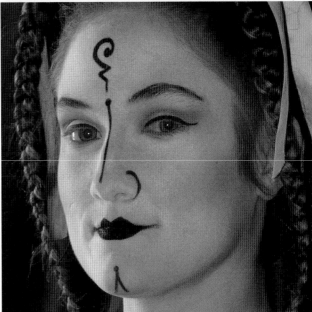

Colin takes his turn sitting in front of the mirror. He is slim, with a youthful-looking face and almost incongruent beard. As we talk he divides the beard into five ponytails with rubber bands. Clown white face paint goes on next, then giant blue and orange triangles around his eyes.

"I started juggling when I was living in Prague," he says. "I met a bunch of street performers there and hung out with them and eventually went to Holland with them for this festival. I met a family there—a professional juggler with his wife and kids—and actually got a job as their nanny. So I moved in with them in Belgium, and when the youngest kid was in school during the day I'd practice juggling up in the attic."

Colin's main act for this show is a straightforwardly charming park scene in which he juggles a doll along with the regular pins, eventually throwing the doll up into a tiny chair balanced on a long pole that is in turn balanced on his head. Colin generates a sort of joyous emotion with his doll juggling partner: when it flies up into the chair the entire audience cheers; when the two huddle together on a park bench for a good night's sleep a collective "awwww" accompanies the fading stage lights.

He came up with the skit, and wrote the music for it and welded the park bench and lamppost set himself, after his two other longtime juggling partners quit the group. "It's been interesting," he says. "There's a lot more pressure when you're out there on your own juggling because—"his large brown eyes glancing up significantly—"obviously when you drop it's *you*. When there's three people out there, if you drop or someone else drops, stuff is going on and you cover together. It doesn't seem quite so *damaging*.

"But I'm happy. One of my main goals was to get a five-club juggle in there and I think I've been pretty consistent with that. I've been working on that almost since I started juggling and it's just now finally starting to come together. There's nothing like doing something in performance to make you sort of panic into being able to do it. You ask some famous juggler, 'When did you finally feel like five clubs was ready for performance?' and he'll say, 'After I performed it for three months.'

"I've got a little story going on with my doll. I'm not an extremely technical juggler. I have my moments but I'd never play Las Vegas doing an eight-minute solid juggling routine, you know? So I kind of mix it up with the whole story of the doll and the scene in the park to make it a little more like a story that people will grasp on to. Throwing him up into the chair is a pretty fun trick . . . I like the fact that the doll is the highest thing on stage. It has this feeling to it— and it probably seems more difficult than it really is. It's more of a trick in the goofy category than a trick in the strictly technical category."

Jason/Dr. Calamari, a former wildlife rehabilitation worker, is sitting on the vintage green couch imitating open-mouthed baby birds in his white-face makeup. He and Evelyn Bittner, a veterinarian, began acrobalancing together just two years ago. After initially providing technical assistance to the circus, they apprenticed themselves to a pair of gymnastics coaches who agreed to begin training them as performers.

"It's the most fun, rewarding thing I've ever done," says Jason. "You know I've always loved the circuses. It never occurred to me that I could actually do it, especially once I reached a certain age. I was thirty-seven and I was thinking 'You know, I'm just at a point in my life where there are certain things that I'm never gonna do.' And one of the examples I had in my head was 'Well, I'm probably never going to run away and join the circus.'" He laughs gleefully. "It was just a few months after that that I ran away and joined the circus."

When it's time for the show to begin, the crowd at the Navy base is bulging. Three rows of people are allowed to sit crosslegged on the floor, in front of the bleachers, while more are standing in back. Dozens more have to be turned away. In a loft above the stage, the band members begin to take their places: Greg with his accordion; Joe Albanese (Dexter Mantooth), bassist, wearing a plumed admiral's hat; Sari Breznau (Pinky d'Ambrosia), trumpet, looking coquettish in cowgirl getup; Matt Manges (Bunny LaMonte), drums, in a red bunny suit; and Kevin Hinshaw (Chameleo), clarinet, in a bowler hat and vest. The bunny strikes up a rousing march, ears resolutely flopping in time to the strident beat, while Kevin hunches over his clarinet. Kevin, whose curly black hair gives him boyish good looks, almost transforms in performance, with a hunch that develops behind his shoulders and a screwed-up face. Someone is heard to ask, "Who's that funny little man on the end?"

Armitage Shanks, the Bombastic Circus Barker, bursts onto the stage as the other performers march together to the center. He sings a welcome to the audience in a minor key, and the cast members introduce themselves one by one. After that, it's on to a dance number

about witch-burning called "Marshmallows and a Holy Bible," as old woodcuts depicting Middle Age torture scenes roll on a back screen. Dr. Calamari drives his nefarious wagon on to the scene and tosses a syringe to the unsuspecting Acrophelia. Stunt-bunny Bunny LaMonte sets up a hilarious game of "target" with an audience volunteer who is supposed to throw tennis balls at various targets throughout the show. The girl cast members do another dance number, this time to speakeasy jazz, wearing vintage slips and bowler hats, and Jenny Iacobucci (Colin's girlfriend) does a few basic hat tricks, leaning over and flipping the bowler held behind her up on to her head.

In a blood-splattered butcher's apron, Armitage Shanks sings a grisly song, "The Slaughter's Promenade." A sort of Tom Waits demi-urge manifesting on the upper stage with the band, his bloody apron draped over pants made out of a U.S. flag, he slowly builds to a literally quaking frenzy as he grinds out the lyrics ("What an effervescent tone the cows make when they scream…"), abruptly switching at the end to the friendly falsetto of a McDonald's employee taking an order.

A beautiful aerial act by Lara's protégé, Kari Nelson, on the tissu is followed by Dr. Calamari's encounter with the life-size puppet of his dear, departed Acrophelia. The stunt bunny returns for another go at taunting the audience with a variety of targets. And then it's time for insect-taming.

A giant deep sea earthworm "capable of withstanding temperatures exceeding 5,000° F but not terribly bright" slinks on to the stage, looking suspiciously like a human being sewn up in a long sack. Lara, in a shiny black leather Ringmistress ensemble and whip, persuades the stubborn invertebrate to jump through a hoop. A tall flesh-eating fly "known to leave up to 30,000 eggs at a time in the festering wounds of humans and animals" appears next, sporting delicate wings and a white ruffled collar reminiscent of a sixteenth century Dutch burgher. The Ringmistress corrals the fly. "Leopold, tell the nice ladies and gentlemen how old you are." The fly taps a leg three times. Fanfare and applause. But the real star emerges next: a giant Amazonian dung beetle "weighing up to 170 kilograms and able to reduce two small children to bones in just under three minutes." The dung beetle is nearly six feet tall including its enormous, stag-like pincers, and is wearing a slick, black vinyl dress with slits on both sides to reveal it's surprisingly shapely legs. The Ringmistress daringly places her head between its pincers. All three insects hop up and pose on mini platforms. The applause is now boundless.

"Yes ladies and gentlemen, the Backstreet Boys don't have *this* in their show!" growls Armitage Shanks. The first act comes to an end as the grey tail of the deep sea earthworm slips underneath the curtain.

* * *

At the circus house, a pianist is plodding through a ragtime melody that I am on the verge of loathing after hearing it for the fifteenth (or is it the twentieth?) time. Five circus members, plus the pianist, live here in this old two-story residence near a city lake. I'm waiting to meet the troupe for the first time while their roommate, who was planting blueberry bushes in the back yard when I first arrived, now practices on the upright piano in the front parlor, sending chords ringing through the otherwise empty house. The same half-dark Seattle grey that has filled the house all afternoon is still coming in the windows as evening approaches. There is a comfortably musty smell in the parlor. Two thin but well-illustrated books are sitting on the sofa nearest the piano: "Flies: From Flower Flies to Mosquitoes" and "Insects."

Nothing is quite so grating on the nerves as the practice of ragtime, I decide. Framed posters of the Bindlestiff Family Cirkus and the New Pickle Family Circus adorn the pea-green walls. The six people living here buy groceries jointly, sharing household responsibilities via a chore wheel posted in the kitchen. The pianist stops (thankfully) to take a call from their food co-op. The group does not like the currently available flavor of organic granola—could they please get some other kind? he asks.

When he returns we strike up a conversation. The pianist says that for him the circus is about play—the rediscovery and affirmation of play—much more than it is about skill. "Cirque du Soleil is about skill, to a level where it almost doesn't seem human. But when Circus Contraption performs you can almost see yourself up there. It's you that's playing even though they're the ones up there doing all the work."

I begin writing in my notebook as he vanishes to another part of the house: "Therein lies the key to why I love these homemade performances even more than acts such as Cirque du Soleil—because it is me that is there, that is playing, that is

clowning, that is clearly running away from reality. It is *that* that I love, the raw desire to subvert the drudgery of ordinary order, which is not even recognized for its dreariness until a tightrope walker with a blue umbrella magically appears dancing above a street corner to confound all notions of common sense. It sends us smiling and laughing back into the everyday, smiling complicitly in our knowledge that this, too, is play, that we've made the whole thing up, the world of phenomenon."

The next night I am only partly surprised when, after the show, Lara finds a blue umbrella and begins twirling it around for the entertainment of friends who have stayed to help clean up. While other circus members are pushing brooms and putting away promotional merchandise and hauling the donated keg of beer back to a truck, the blue umbrella twirls . . . a playful talisman, accomplishing on its own the daring trapeze leap from imagination to reality.

Back at the circus house, Colin and Jenny are the first troupe members to come through the front door on our initial evening together. The two have been romantically attached for eight years since meeting in Prague, where Jenny worked in English-language theater and Colin eventually returned to do street juggling. Jenny is elfish-looking: short with dark blond hair in two pigtails. She plays the dung beetle in performance, although she admits that the costume, which has no eyeholes, doesn't really allow her to see, so she stumbles blindly around on stage at her cue. The pair begin discussing the ingenious design of a friend's hand puppet and decide spontaneously to make one. They go down to the house's cellar—an immense tangle of junk—and happily begin rooting around for pieces of wood and an appropriate saw.

David/Armitage Shanks arrives home next, his third home to share with the circus. "When we first started off Lara and I were living in Ballard (a Seattle neighborhood)," he says. "We knocked a hole in the ceiling and put her trapeze up in a room about this big." (He motions to the size of the front parlor.) "It was sitting three feet off the ground and that's where she'd practice, in our living room. Then we moved to a loft warehouse in Freemont and we built a little riser for storage and props, so basically the circus was living in our house for a year and a half and we'd rehearse in the parking lot. We'd haul all our crap out and set up and rehearse there. All the local business people would be out smoking and watching us; the people from the local coffeehouse would come down.

"We started to define roles, and had endless meetings over minutiae, deciding what kind of gigs we wanted—'We don't want to work for Camel but we will work for Bob's Car Thing'—and getting all the personalities together... It was like traffic school. We were having meetings to talk about when our next meetings were going to be and for a while it was just evil. A lot of it was getting used to creating a society together and creating your own political body.

"We're a paradigm of community, a paradigm of family," David continues. "I think it's increasingly important, as things become more commodified and stratified, that we be something more than professionals showing up for rehearsal. We're all living here because we feel the benefit in creating our own family. We moved here specifically for that reason, so that we can constantly talk about [the circus]. It's almost impossible for us to go anywhere outside and not continue the dialogue."

David is the primary organizer of the band, which is an integral part of the circus. Performers switch back and forth between the main stage and the second-story band alcove. The juggler plays trombone, the trumpet player dances, the stunt-bunny plays drums and the aerialist is learning the tuba. "I have a lot of theoretical background in music," says David. "I'll come in with something in my head and say, 'I want this to sound like a rusty Chevy with three tires,' and Greg, who's got a great ear for songwriting, will turn it into a true song. When Sari and Kevin came on board, they were then able to take a song and make great arrangements."

And the dark quality whence come such lyrics as "What an effervescent tone the cows make when they scream . . . "?

"That's actually from an old Mister Rogers show . . . ha ha!!! It was great seeing your face when I said that," teases David. "Okay kids, can you say 'effervescent?' That song in particular came out of a New York Times full-page ad from PETA that described what happens in a slaughterhouse. But my background influences are things like cabaret, Tom Waits, old world horror—not like a film—but Edward Gorey, that type of thing. I've written other things such as "July like a Dog," which is a pretty fun drinking song. But I found my natural tendency to be these dark allegories. I wanted to deal with both fantastical surreal dream stuff and this dark German cabaret-esque vibe. It's a place that leaves a lot of room for exposition. Particularly in a circus context, you have something to create from if there's a story there—it gives you some legs. My other natural inclination was to write self-effacing songs about my relationships with women I went to college with or something—it might not have as much legs for us to try to do something. One song literally came out of Lara saying, 'Wouldn't it be cool if we made giant insects and a giant beetle? Would you write a song about beetles?' I guess our natural proclivities is what shapes the music."

The next day finds Jenny sitting at the breakfast table, perusing a letter from the mayor of the city of Lynnwood informing the group they have been officially banned from performing in that particular Seattle suburb. Enclosed with the letter are samples of communications the mayor's office received after Circus Contraption did a children's show in Lynnwood a few months earlier. An excerpt from one:

Dear Chief of Police, Lynnwood Police Department,

White facial makeup with black lipstick . . . {is} macabre. {As for} the Beetlejuice outfit for the MC, Beetlejuice is supposedly some Satan figure . . . Any careful adult knows better than to expose children to entertainment that can be called tripe. Taxpayers are offended when taxes pay for morally unclean things. I am legally mandated to report this to you because I have an active R.N. license and I think my job's done. I felt abused . . . like it was being forced on me. I felt THAT NOT OK FEELING . . .

The letter goes on further to object to the presence of a "dragon" with a flickering tongue (it was actually a puppet giraffe), to Dr. Calamari and Acrophelia's necrobalancing act, and a shadow puppet skit in which animals escape from the zoo and go drinking in bars.

Another letter writer reports to the authorities the unwholesome fact that one of the performers—horrors!—*smelled bad.*

"The irony," Colin says, "is that we used to have a member of the troupe who was one of those never-bathe hippie types; he would sometimes get pretty rancid. But he wasn't with us by that show."

The show in question was one in which the circus had removed its adult-themed numbers and changed lyrics on others to be suitable to the younger audience. What the indignant letter writers seem to object to, therefore, is not really any particularly offensive subject or act, but to an aesthetic that presents, in an original and humorous way, an undercurrent running through all circus both mainstream and alternative. As pure imagery, white-faced clowns and ringmasters with whips bear a connection with the underworld. Circus Contraption deliberately exploits such images with skill, maintaining the vital element of play that enables the audience to participate in, and laugh at, even the darkest, most chthonic aspects of our own subterranean realms.

Interestingly enough, as more members of the circus make their way into the kitchen this morning, not one person questions the legal right of the mayor of Lynnwood to banish them for the heinous crime of wearing black lipstick and failing to appeal to the rigid tastes of a small group of suburbanites. Instead, inevitably, they want to know what the official dictionary definition of "tripe" is. Webster's is pulled down from a shelf and left out for consultation on the breakfast table. Pancakes are casually served. Jenny, with the letters spread around her, begins writing a skit lampooning the situation, showing the circus members behind bars while a frumpy housewife quotes directly from their Lynnwood fan mail.

The difference between mainstream circus and Circus Contraption, David says later, is aesthetic choice.

"The primacy for us is doing what moves us and what we feel compelled to create," he says. "The primacy for [mainstream circus] is putting together this whole package that's going to sell—and that's not bad. They're always thinking, 'Is this going to be cool for everyone? How much of this do we need to dumb down to make sure everyone gets it?' . . . so consequently you get a certain mainstream outlook. For us, we do what we do. And there have been shows, like at an elementary school, where we have to change the lyrical content. We laugh about it, but it kind of sucks that we're changing what we do. Currently we make sure that everyone knows there's mature content in this show. Kevin went as far as to call back people who had phoned in reservations to make sure they knew of the adult content, which is a lot farther than a lot of us would have gone, but we appreciated he did it. It's like 'You are coming to *our* world.' If you're bringing your nine-year-old, it's because you're a cool parent and we expect you'll have a full dialogue with your kid . . . or you'll walk out and that's okay too."

Circus Contraption calls itself "A Bracing Curative for the Afflictions of Our Times," a slogan that covers their posters and T-shirts and sounds as if it might easily have been peeled off the back of a turn-of-the-century medicine bottle left in the wake of a Baptist tent revival. They earn the epithet through explorations of subconscious, subterranean, and occasionally dark imagery that result in healing laughter, in addition to awe-inspiring physical demonstrations of skill (as on Lara's trapeze). But there is also the attempt to create community and family and to elevate play to a sort of guiding life principle—witness the thirty-seven-year-old turned acrobat or the advanced degree holders (there are several master's and PhD's in the group) now putting their intellectual talents to the task of, say, designing giant insects. One recent college graduate and member of the group says she gets "a certain satisfaction from mending old stockings rather than buying new ones."

But beyond skill and commitment is the ongoing sense that all of this is achievable, is within the grasp of all that are human. Witness the song "The Entertainer" . . . as performed on beer bottles. David explains:

"One of the things that continually pleases me and encapsulates a certain quality of what we are is the beer bottles. Partly because it literally came out of a party here after one of the shows; we were all sitting around drinking beer and sodas, talking, laughing and all of a sudden someone "hoof"—"he makes a blowing sound—"and someone else, and all of a sudden it's an idea.

"There are lots of transcendent moments in the show, but the beer bottles for me is one because there's nothing to it. We're all together, there's nothing going on, there's no guile, there's no big act. We've traditionally done it at the end of the show. We all come together and the lights come up. The audience sees us for who we are and what we are: we're people getting together and working together for four years trying to do this thing. We're standing around and we play this beautiful music on *beer bottles*.

"To me, all the time, I think, 'This is it; this is so righteous and holy and good.'"

2

zam ora

The

TORTURE KING

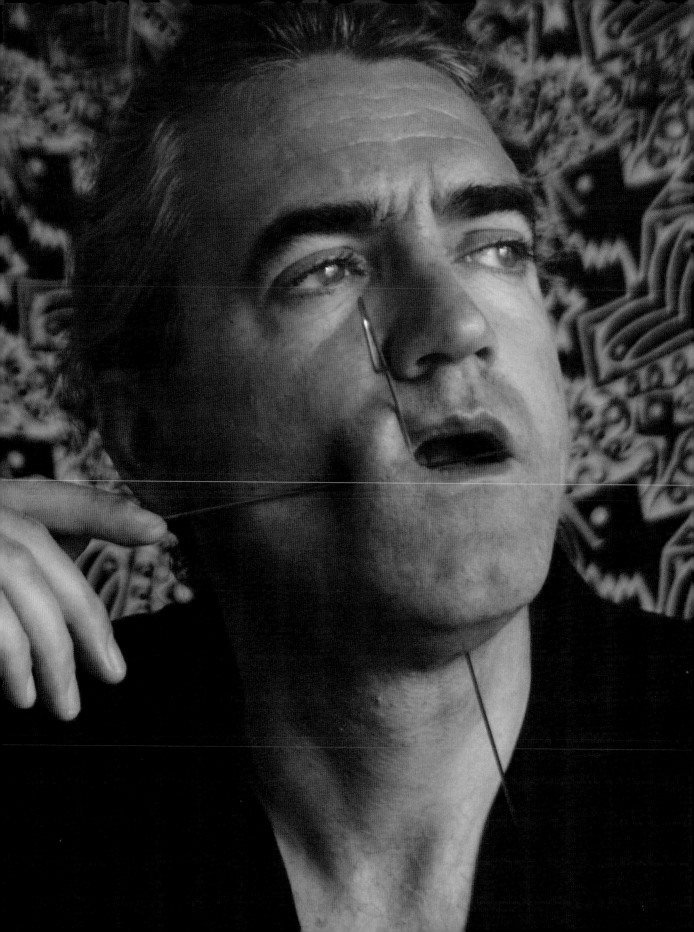

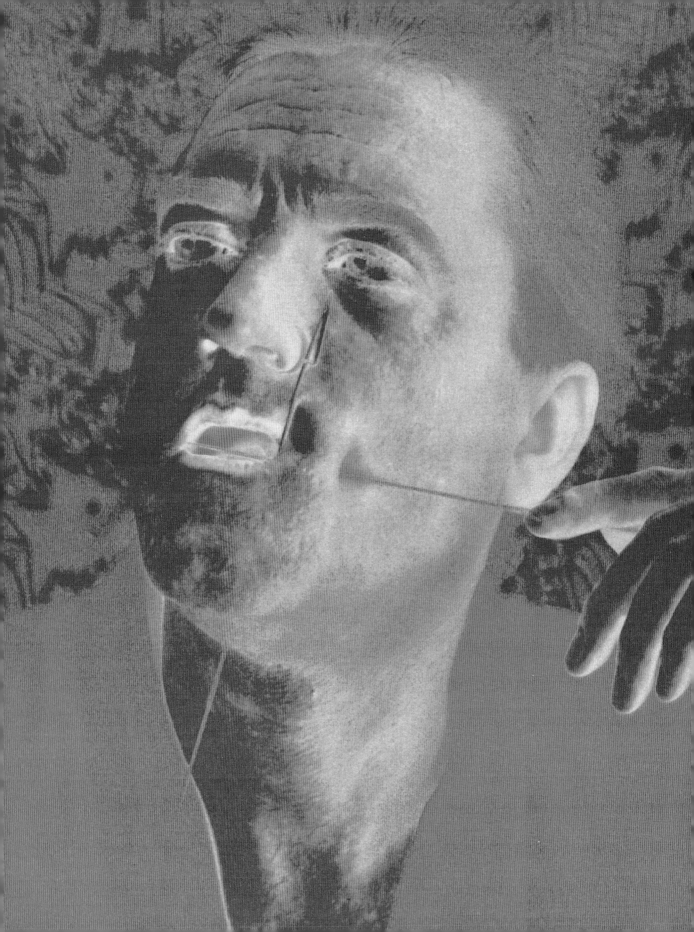

TIM CRIDLAND IS poking around inside of his mouth, under his tongue, searching for a decent entry point. His right hand holds an eight-inch long steel skewer, custom-made at a friend's piercing salon. He pushes, his left hand massaging the area under his chin, helping to coax the trajectory of a newly created pathway leading from the tender, slick membranous lining under the tongue, all the way through to the roughened skin under his jaw. His face screws up, not with pain but with concentration. His heavy black eyebrows crush themselves to the center of his forehead, his eyes roll up, his chin begins to rise in the direction of the ceiling. Underneath the jawline, a little triangle of skin, lifted like a small tent by the prodding of the skewer, dances around, seeking its point of exit. Suddenly, crisply, the bright steel tip emerges, piercing the canvas of skin. It's a new hole—the one that he made earlier this evening in front of an audience gleams a full inch to the left of the new hole, blood still drying around its circular edges. There is no visible blood at the site of the new wound as Tim pushes further, the skewer now extending from past his nose, down into his mouth and out again to graze his collarbone. This is the third time I've seen him perform this stunt but the first time that I know, beyond a shadow of a doubt, that he's not just hyping an unusual piercing. I take the opportunity to approach closer and tell Tim, with the most awe I can possibly manifest, "You're the real deal."

His hazel eyes have returned from the ceiling to their normal plane of focus. Tim smiles carefully, his slightly gapped front teeth tapping against the metal skewer protruding out of his mouth. "The real deal, am I?" he says, still with an awkward smile. He is trying to talk without moving his mouth, but otherwise appears entirely comfortable.

He is Zamora—the Torture King.

His is possibly the most physically extreme act touring the country today. The Torture King also puts skewers directly through his biceps and through the muscles of his forearms, along with a host of smaller surgical needles through the skin of his chest. All in a night's work.

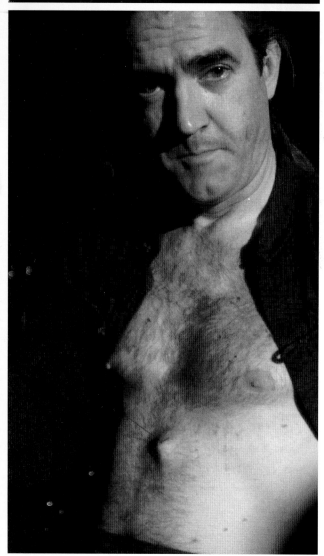

He holds the Guinness Book record for the most live piercings—one hundred—at a single time. "I could easily have done more," Tim adds, but the Guinness TV show producers thought that was about as much as their intended audience could stand. At live shows, faintings are not uncommon.

He eats lightbulbs, swallows swords, walks on broken glass and once even had a 2,500-pound Toyota drive over him while he was lying on a bed of nails. None of these feats are "gaffes," the sideshow lingo for tricks or illusions. But inevitably it's the needles that evoke groans from the audience, cause fingernails to dig into palms and invite foreheads to hit the floor. As Tim determinedly works a skewer through his upper left arm, the onlookers gasp and yell, "No, no, NO! That is so WRONG!"

Tim, a.k.a. Zamora, was the original stickman of the Jim Rose Circus, and continues to make a living out of impaling himself like a shish-kebab on sharp objects. When I catch up with Tim in February 2003, he's found himself a temporary home as the star of an off-beat Las Vegas show called "Shock"—a sort of variation on "Fear Factor" with comedy and sex appeal thrown in.

Shock takes place in a cabaret-sized theater inside of the Bourbon Street Hotel & Casino, a joint that, to put it kindly, has seen better days. Stale cigarette air vies with the smell of lemon antiseptic in the lobby and hallways. In the public bathrooms, toilet bowls still bear retail stickers from another era proclaiming their "Sanitizing SWISHER action!" alongside toilet paper holders covered with multiple brown cigarette burns. Scarred carpets, scratched mirrors and constant low-grade pandemonium from a bank of attention-seeking slot machines complete the picture. One positive: the hotel is one of the few on the Strip still carrying on the declining Las Vegas tradition of $2.99 breakfasts and $7 steak-and-lobster dinners.

The show is "four-walling" here—renting the space and paying for its own advertising without assistance from the hotel. Tim is hopeful. "A lot of well-known acts have started here and then moved on to play bigger venues," he says. He sits beside me on a stool in front of a slot machine, wearing jeans and a black T-shirt. At thirty-nine, his formerly dark brown, waist-length ponytail has gone mostly grey, a noticeable change from the photos of his starting days a decade ago with the Jim Rose circus. His eyes under the thick brows are hypnotic; his cheeks famously hold a set of dimples created by his former routine of cheek-to-cheek skewering. He doesn't perform that particular piercing anymore, he says, because people often assume he has a permanent piercing there. In reality, the dimples are caused by built-up scar tissue.

The King of Pain was born in Pullman, Washington, to a pair of English immigrants. His father, a botany professor, owned a toy shop during Tim's developing years; his mother is described as an eccentric recluse. The youthful Tim became interested in esoteric subjects after reading a book in his elementary school library that described strange acts around the world, such as Indian snake charming and sideshow sword-swallowers. "I kept the interest and it just kind of turned into a weird hobby," he explains.

From there it was on to fire eating in his early teens, and some other typical sideshow acts garnered from a hippie street performer by the name of Reverend Chumley.

His first public piercing took place at age fifteen, in school, during a home economics class. "I started lifting the skin of my forearms and piercing it with sewing pins," Tim says. "I was told by the teacher to stop."

He continued experimenting in private with pins and needles, but didn't consider what he was doing as a potential "act" until he saw a flyer for the Jim Rose circus, then performing in Seattle. Tim and his friend Paul Lawrence, both in their early twenties, showed up to see "Jimmy the Geek" eat broken glass at a local club. Tim had another friend, Matt, who had a gross trick of drinking liquids through a tube put down his nose. Matt thought it was just a funny bar stunt—but Tim envisioned a stage act. All three joined Jim Rose and ended up on board the first-ever national Lollapalooza tour of 1992, in which their combined sick-o talents made headlines everywhere from *Rolling Stone* to local gazettes.

Back in the hotel lobby Tim and I are joined by Joel, a similarly black-clad youth in his early twenties who has become a fan of Shock. He plans to help take tickets tomorrow night while in drag, to add to the show's freaky ambience. He's a professional body piercer and, naturally, an appreciator of the Torture King.

"I've pierced myself about 150 times over the years," Joel says. "I've sewn my legs together. And I still don't understand how Tim does what he does through muscle." The two of them discuss their favorite piercing music: Joel exclusively listens to Skinny Puppy during his needling sessions while Tim prefers Dead Can Dance.

Tim was already performing the most extreme of his piercings by the time he joined Jim Rose. His first muscle piercing—through the mouth and out the chin—took place in the Santa Cruz manufacturing studio of the same friend who made him his surgical-grade steel skewers.

"I had researched the one through the chin through photographs of this mystic group in Jordan that does incredible body demonstrations. I was kind of basing it on that," Tim recalls. During the first insertion, "I could feel my blood, veins and arteries through the muscle. I was very aware of that. It was pretty intense."

His vitals demonstrate that Tim is processing sensations differently, rather than simply suppressing his reactions. His muscles relax, his heart rate drops. Because of this, he hardly bleeds at all in performance. On the second night we catch Shock, Tim's right forearm begins oozing crimson after his usual skewer insertion. He calmly applies pressure onstage while receiving applause for the act. Later he notes that it was the first time in almost a year that he had experienced noticeable bleeding.

The show itself is equal parts campy fun and horrific. On the camp side is a girl in a microscopic nurse outfit singing Oingo Boingo's "Dead Man's Party" while slinking about a male audience member lashed to an electric chair. On the horrific is a hypnosis segment in which another audience volunteer puts his head in a cage full of rats while under the impression he is receiving a face and scalp massage. A combination attraction is "The King": a man who lifts a bowling ball with a hook attached to his pierced penis. Throughout appears the Torture King—eating lightbulbs, walking on glass and cutting open his abdomen with a scalpel to pull out a string that he has allegedly ingested.

Tim takes his work—and it's sociocultural origins—very seriously, and seems almost a little apologetic as he preps us for "Shock" in the lobby of the Bourbon Street. "It's not the kind of show I would normally do," he mentions more than once. But afterwards he agrees that the combination of comedy, curvaceous women and sideshow stunts makes a more interesting ride for the audience than one long, tension-filled parade of horrors. Weekend after weekend, the black-curtained showroom is patronized by a young, hip crowd eager to walk a few blocks off the Las Vegas strip to see something unusual. Tim hangs around afterwards, genially answering questions from fans, even with a large skewer poking out of his face.

One afternoon, Tim shows me the hotel room that has become his regular weekend home, spending a few minutes first to rearrange his possessions before the arrival of a visitor. The tiny roomlet is almost engulfed by a normal-sized bed with a garish, red-patterned bedcover. A little plug-in cooking burner—the staple accessory of a traveling performer—perches on a dresser top. At the foot of the bed, a large plastic box contains his videotapes and promotional materials.

A connoisseur of Las Vegas-on-the-cheap, Tim leads me to his favorite haunts around the Strip. First there is the free acrobatics and belly-dancing display at Aladdin's Palace. While waiting for the show to begin, the Torture King investigates a variety of aromatherapy oils at The Body Shop next door. He has decided he wants to make his room at the Bourbon Street "more like home," and finally settles on a ceramic candleholder and set of two blended oils. It seems weirdly cute that the Torture King appreciates such refinements as essential oils. Apparently even a painmeister enjoys some creature comforts.

After the Aladdin, we hike down Las Vegas Blvd. to the Flamingo. It's a perfect day, sunny and cool, with purplish desert mountains on the horizon serving as a sort of distant reality check to the outlandish casino architecture lining the Strip. At the Flamingo there's a free aerial show over the main casino floor. Two bare-chested, buff Tarzans swing on the ceiling while a master of ceremonies and team of dancing girls work the stage on top of the slot machines. After a short time of appreciating this cornucopia of kitsch, we move to the (also free) Las Vegas Museum, where Tim spends a long time watching a TV loop documenting the mob's influence in Sin City. Mob activity and conspiracy theories are among his favorite interests, some of which he has written about and published in his own 'zine, *Off the Deep End*.

"I have a broad range of subjects I'm interested in," Tim says. "People paint their own pictures of what I'm about. But people who know me know that basically I'm just into different information."

All the time I am walking around with the Torture King, I keep thinking that someone will stop and look at him, ask for his autograph or even bow down. Jim Rose, his former sideshow coworker and consummate barker, used to orchestrate a delightful moment during the old show when the entire audience would make mock obeisance

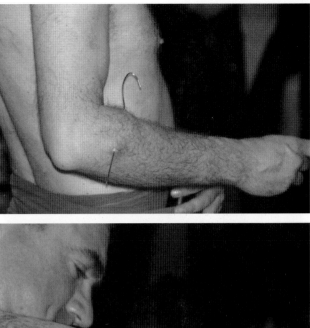

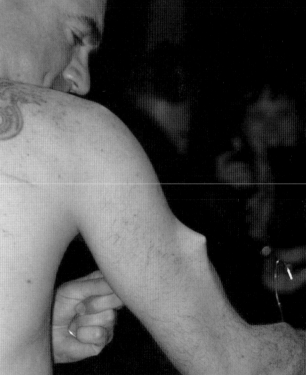

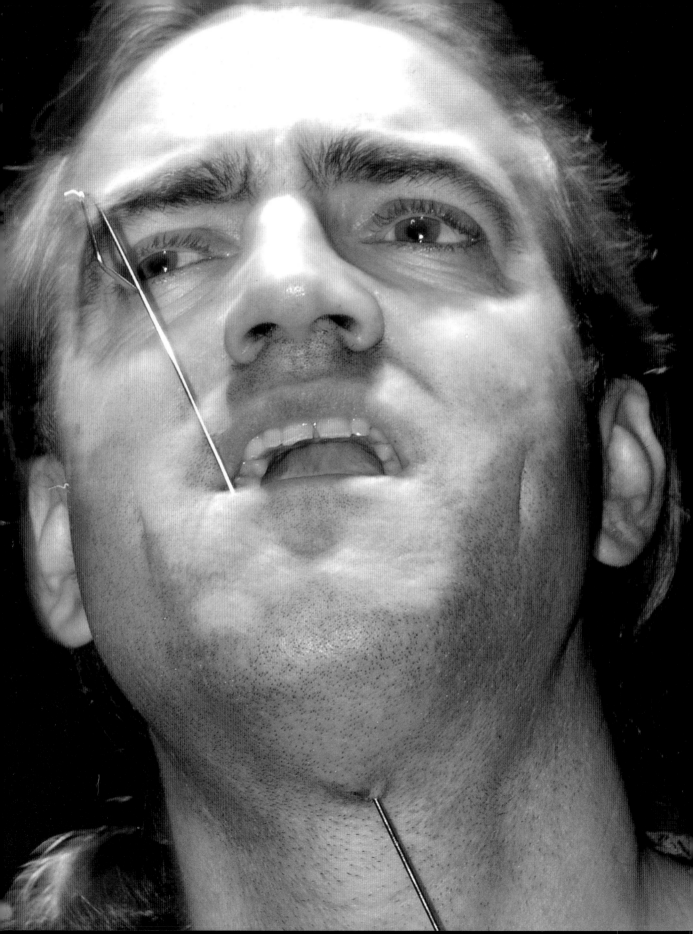

before Tim. "Your KING!!!" Rose, practically apoplectic, would hoarsely thunder to the delighted crowd, which responded with waves of bowing arms and torsos.

Nothing like this happens here in Las Vegas. Tim looks pretty normal in street clothes, with no permanent piercings or visible tattoos. Unless he happens to speak, that is, and then one notices . . . the tongue.

Which is split. In two.

Tim, to borrow the Native American phrase, "speaks with forked tongue." The two divergent points delicately indicate separate directions whenever he speaks, almost as a visual encouragement to consider both sides of whatever he happens to be saying.

It's a rare body mod that only a few people in the country have had performed, usually with the assistance of an extraordinarily open-minded oral surgeon. Tim, on the other hand, split his tongue himself. "I just ran some fishing line through the hole where I had my tongue piercing, and gradually, maybe over a period of about three weeks, I pulled it down," Tim says. He adds modestly, "It took some dedication."

"People always say things like 'I have a high pain threshold,'" he says. "But not a lot thought of them have thought about *why* they have a high pain threshold. I began to think 'how did I teach myself to do what I do?' And I realized it was a process that can be taught."

Part of his training came from an unlikely source: a group of spiritual practitioners known as Sufis, which represents a mystically derived branch of Islam. He spent some time in 1994 studying with the Qadiri-Rifai, a Sufi training group in California.

"A lot of people don't understand what a *fakir* is," Tim says. "They think of Hindus purposely putting themselves in a state of discomfort, like holding their hand over their head for a year . . . but Sufis are actually in a state of protection. I'm not trying to overcome pain, I'm protected from it."

Tim later posts this explanation to an online sideshow discussion group: "Fakir is an Arabic word that means 'someone who has nothing.' It means that everything in life is temporary, and a fakir is someone who realizes this. Most fakirs do not do feats of pain control and self-injury. Most just sing and dance. The most commonly know type of fakir is the Whirling Dervish. The group of fakirs that are most known for acts of self-injury are called Rafias. They are followers of the Sufi 'saint' of healing Ahmed ar Rifai. They are commonly referred to as Howling Dervishes. They do not do these things to get into a spiritual state, they are already in a spiritual state before they do these feats. The state that they are in protects them from the injuries and pain. There is no endorphin rush. Although the feats may be seen as examples of self-injury, they could be more accurately described as acts of self-healing, as there is minimal injury and rapid healing associated with the feats. I'm sure this will lead to more discussion . . . ."

Ken Harck, owner/operator of the Brothers Grim Sideshow, has engaged Tim several times to perform with his traveling historical sideshow and has this to say: "In the entire history of the sideshow, he's the best act ever. For some reason, a certain percentage of people think he's some punk masochist. But what he's really showing is mind over matter. He should be an inspiration to anyone who wants to overcome something in life."

Several TV crews have tried to document the "secret" of Tim's almost superhuman resistance to pain, although he readily admits that a disciplined mind and meditative techniques are his two major means. As he said earlier, "Some parts of pain are a learned response and you can teach yourself how to react to it over time." He has even generated some interest in the medical community in areas that involve long-term pain management.

Not long ago, one enterprising crew from the Discovery Channel brought Tim into the office of a pain clinic at UCLA. "They actually hooked me to a 'pain–inducing machine'—boy was I thrilled when they told me," Tim says. (He doesn't *like* pain, you see, he just knows how to reinterpret it.) A heating element was taped to the back of his hand, and instructions were given him to press one button when awareness was felt and another to signal pain. Without any intention to do so, he ran the meter all the way to the top and was *still waiting* for the pain to begin when a surprised doctor informed him the test was over.

"I was actually expecting a lot more pain," Tim recalls cheerfully. "But now I have a scientific statement that says I process pain in a different way than most people do."

The sun is glowing orange on the western horizon by the time we turn and head back up the Strip to the hotel. Tim stops in a drugstore to buy a lightbulb to eat later on during that night's show. Snacktime in the hardware section. He has to get back to start sterilizing his needles in the pressure cooker he uses as a makeshift autoclave.

I ask him about his relationship to the underground scene of body modifiers, performance piercers and meathook danglers.

"A lot of people are doing piercing because it has become its own tribe. Me, I was always the type to be expelled from the counterculture," he says with a slight laugh, briefly revealing both teeth and forked tongue. "I've been making a living for the last decade as a professional *fakir*. The modern primitives don't know how to be entertaining. Most piercing performances are just this kind of gross, blood and saliva stuff."

"I'm kind of a guy without a tribe," Tim says, returning to a theme. "At first I thought I might get some people together who were interested in the same things. But what actually happens is people get into this just from the point of view of getting the tribe together, and that is maybe more important to them than the show itself. It just degenerates into a party scene with people drunk onstage. And the show business part of me says that you've got to do something for the audience."

When he organized his last group road tour, he says, "people were like 'teach me this, do this for me' . . . I had a fantasy that everyone would uplift each other, but it was more people getting brought down. I was doing way more work and getting much less appreciation. I was doing the booking, the publicity, I was the main performer and the emcee, *and* I was driving and handling the finances—and these guys come just wanted to come on board and party. They were more into the idea of it than the reality."

"I guess my own tribe would be Sufi people, kind of. But lately I've been more into doing stuff alone."

Alone, or letting someone else handle the particulars of putting a show together that incorporates his truly bizarre body demonstrations as the main draw. Maybe Las Vegas could be the terrestrial Elysium for the Torture King if "Shock" continues its run. He'd like to settle down somewhere, trade in the electric hot plate and let the audience come to *him*. He applies the same confidence to his career as he applies to working a sharp skewer through his upper arm.

"I knew there was a mainstream audience for this."

HER FINGERTIPS ARE blackened with soot, the substance rendered by each evening's performance, each sacral offering. Nadia, the founder of fire troupe Flam Chen, is an exotic-looking woman. A petite 5'2", she wears the front half of her head shaved (the rest hangs in a long brown ponytail), a saffron robe, flowered silk blouse, pink sunglasses and huge lucite hoop hearings. Red Chinese characters are tattooed down the center of her chest. They represent her name: Alev ("little flame"), Nadia ("hope") and Hagen ("comfortable").

We're in a warehouse, just north of downtown Tucson, Arizona. Gesturing with her black fingers, Nadia is sitting across from me, talking about the genesis of Flam Chen. Behind her on the wall, in spray-painted gold letters, are the words "To The Pure All Things Are Pure." This child of New York City—an artist, actor, musician, costume designer and more—equally influenced by both the cultural arts scene of her hometown and the mummy hall of the Natural Museum of History, is the originator of one of the first fire theater groups in the country.

Flam Chen, she says, began in 1995 as an attempt to create a grand finale for an April Fool's Day parade, an event which later became Tucson's annual All Soul's Day procession.

"I was in a performance group [at the time] but I really wanted to work with other performers, dancers and puppeteers, and really pull the community together and do this crazy thing," Nadia says. Almost to her surprise, she and two others received a community arts grant for the purpose.

An idea developed to have two enormous dragons, covered with rose-petal scales and with live performers inside spitting fire out of the mouths. Nadia knew of a few fire-breathers in town who enthusiastically agreed to collaborate.

The public response to this first-time experiment surpassed expectation. "I was amazed," recalls Nadia. "We had thousands and thousands of people just pour out into the streets. The other thing that was so amazing was what we got away with . . . . We got to spit huge flames

in the middle of downtown and set up fire installations and had torches just lining the street. The fire marshall was completely unimpressed by a six-foot spit."

"We kind of went, 'Wow—we can get away with anything!'"

The fire performers who had been in the procession began meeting on a regular basis to learn and share fire tricks, and began thinking up ways of incorporating them into other types of performance—and Flam Chen was born. They staged elaborately choreographed pieces featuring flaming sets, fire props, and lit costume pieces. By the late nineties, it was not entirely unusual to see other fire performers spinning poi—two lit balls on the ends of chains—at open-air concerts and alternative festivals across the country. But very few possessed the skills to do what Flam Chen was doing in 1995. Certainly no one was doing it with giant ten-foot puppets, operatic sets, and poetic vision.

Jess Daniels was a 21-year-old activist, hopping trains to San Francisco for Chinese New Year, when he stopped in Tucson just a few weeks before that first downtown procession. A Romanian street performer who was going to be in one of the dragons taught him how to spit fire. He ended up performing in the parade.

It was admittedly exciting to send huge balls of flame into the air over the heads of awed spectators. Jess became one of the first regular participants in the group practice sessions, although, as he now points out, "there's no such thing as practice when you're putting fuel in your mouth—it's not 'practice' anymore."

At first, the group just did fire-breathing. Later, after going to Burning Man and seeing the performers there, Flam Chen members were inspired to learn new skills such as staff spinning and fire-eating.

"There was a lot of interesting trial and error at first, for a couple of years," Jess says. "There still is.

"The first time we saw poi we had no idea what was going on. We got these huge lengths of chain—super heavy—and were doing crazy tricks, weaving things in and out of the chain. It was fun. We'd experiment with different kinds of fuel; put them on our arms and light them on fire to see what would work for a transfer and what wouldn't.

"It's pretty interesting, because so much of the stuff that we know how to do I can show someone really quickly now that I've figured out how to do it. But it took a lot of years of figuring it out. And there really weren't that many people doing it then either. When people came through town and had some skills then we'd trade tricks and tips, just check each other out."

To observe a Flam Chen performance is to watch an oracle become possessed; to see human vessels communicating with a primal Spirit. The rapid rise and fall of fire from the spinning poi is simultaneously wild and hypnotic; the audience sits entranced, but with a strange excitement—they feel the desire of the moth for the flame. The fire itself is ever-changing: one moment it is soft and pure, a single tongue sitting atop an oil lamp. In another minute it is furiously kinetic, conjuring wrath and destruction. Fire lends an otherworldly, sacred quality to even the simplest gestures and props. A flaming circle seems to burn with an intent that bespeaks more than its own outline—the entire metaphysical sphere of geometry is speaking through the voice of fire in a loud language that hints but never reveals.

Flam Chen literally reached a new height when Paul Weir joined the troupe in 1998. Paul had spent a lot of time rock-climbing in Yosemite (his home for several years), and had studied suspension systems used in both circus and theater performances. His knowledge of ropes and rigging meant that Flam Chen suddenly became an aerial fire theater.

Again, some experimentation was in order. The nature of Flam Chen's performance meant that the rigging had to be constructed differently than most. All the materials had to burn-proof, and put together in such a way that metal components wouldn't melt or torque under extreme heat.

In 1999 the group was invited to Arcosanti, a world-renowned utopian experiment combining human dwellings with ecology, based in Scottsdale, Arizona. The occasion was the birthday of the architect, eighty-year-old Italian designer Paolo Soleri. Paul got to work drilling holes and planting hooks into the ceiling of "The Vault," a historic forty-foot dome that was used to construct all the other domed structures of Arcosanti.

"Ling Ling," as the performance was called, was a spectacle such as had never been seen before at Arcosanti, or possibly anywhere else. The white-faced fire dancers, bungee cords tied to their ankles, dove from the black depths of the vaulted ceiling, down into the audience with fire in their hands. Trapeze bars—with each end of the bar on fire—enabled them to perform aerial stunts. Below, wearing voluminous white robes, a Flam Chen member inscribed a circle of fire on the ground, then danced in the center holding a gorgeous, flaming fan. Winged creatures and seahorses flew overhead.

The performance was wordless, choreographed only to music, but Nadia later wrote a poem to accompany a series of pictures taken of the event:

> *the daka and dakini show all sorts of marvels*
> *which endless discourses could not equal:*
> *Some with disheveled hair, are stung and fall*
> *others are mounted on sea horses*
> *and wave pennants to the earth*
> *others, ghostly women with dirty hair*
> *have jackals pouring from their mouths*
> *others of human form, with wings*
> *at the level of the sky, make rains*
> *lightening flashes fall and lift their hands*
> *in the standard of the tiger*

The Arcosanti performance tied into another of the group's interests, that of transforming public spaces. Paul in particular, as an industrial designer, butoh performer and installation artist, conceives of Flam Chen almost as another public installation, recalling such times as when the group performed under a Philadelphia bridge one summer. "I like to make people fly in spaces where they don't normally think about flying," he says. "I think about shifting people's consciousness."

Flam Chen is in love with location, even taking risks to perform in places where the atmosphere may be right but an official fire permit is out of the question. In a singular incident that has become legendary amongst the group's followers, Flam Chen once held a secret performance inside a historic old theater that had been closed. They managed to get inside through a forced entry, and found the stage with its old velvet curtains irresistible. An "unofficial" performance was scheduled for a single night only, with invitations sent round by word of mouth. To avoid drawing attention to the event, the audience had to be shuttled from a remote location by van in small groups of about ten. A lookout with a borrowed cell phone stood on top of the building and served as sentry, ready to evacuate the attendees with the first sign of the police. Luckily, the authorities never arrived.

Flam Chen normally rehearses and performs in a state-owned warehouse, part of an entire district in Tucson that has been redeveloped as a zone for non-profit and cultural groups. They share the space with Bikus, a bicycle cooperative that was among the first to combine cycling with community activism and involvement. A spinning whirligig made out of a bicycle wheel and colored reflectors cheerfully decorates the chain link fence at the entryway to Flam Chen's space. Bicycles and bicycle parts lie in scattered piles around the yard.

The space is actually composed of two warehouses: one in which Paul lives and keeps stored materials above the Bikus workshop, and another in which the group actually practices and performs. The latter features a loading dock, which functions nicely as a stage. The giant corrugated metal doors behind it can be raised to reveal an interior stage—or closed to keep out the chill of a desert night when the group is inside practicing.

On a Saturday afternoon, the sounds of hammering, welding and a screaming metal saw erupt from the Bikus workshop. Flam Chen is beginning preparations for this evening's performance, some of them by practicing their poi-spinning in the area in front of the loading dock/stage, others by carefully winding and soaking dozens of wicks in fuel. One of the members, Geneva Foster, sits with her back against the sun-warmed side of the performing warehouse.

"Our biggest potential . . . is the ability to create something that doesn't exist in any other form," she says. "You don't look at this and say this is dance, this is circus, this is butoh or even theater. I think it is very unidentifiable. And when you reach that point of the unknown you can begin to play . . ."

She compares Flam Chen's aesthetic to that of film directors Peter Greenaway and Jean-Pierre Jeunet [*Amelie*]. "They both have a way of using color, narrative, and visuals that creates a sense of magic, of something very pure. It's like a fable.

"What we create is something that is similar but that is actually real, taking place in true time. It's not framed in a box, or given to you in bits of light. But then ironically we are playing with light, and with fire itself adding to that. I like to think we're creating something that makes people step between the lines of categorization."

Flam Chen ranges in performance style from the whimsically accessible (as in the show "Toybox"), to the exotically esoteric. Tonight's show, "The Garden: A Pyrotechnic Allegory," is a good example of the latter. Audience members would be hard-pressed to state exactly what the nature of the allegory is. The story is loosely based on Nadia's reading of the origins of war as taking place in the sacred, original bloodshed of the hunt. The characters of this piece are costumed as warriors and animal spirits. The spirits, with antlers affixed to their heads, dangle overhead waving flaming swords, while the warriors beneath engage in martial displays and eventually shoot the spirits with fiery arrows. As Paul says, the group is becoming "more interested in frames than character." Performances are designed to create visually stunning tableaus that impact an audience more profoundly even than a literal storyline.

Fire "was almost a necessary evil," says Nadia, in creating a powerful visual experience. When Flam Chen first started, she says, fire "wasn't the initial fascination with me. I understood that if I wanted to get this [effect] that I would have to be cool with it; I would have to find some place within myself where I was comfortable. It's almost like martial arts: the danger ups the challenge but it's not the motivation."

Danger is certainly ever-present. Paul recalls a time when he was performing in the "Toybox" show. In it, two performers on stilts wear giant, six-foot steel hoop skirts, out of which various characters emerge through a door in the front of each skirt. One night, Paul came out dressed in his character of a toy soldier. In the waistband of his pants he had stuffed flash paper to be used later in the show. But as he played his drums, the heat created on the drum heads apparently ignited all the flash paper at once: a huge explosion went off around his body. Paul, in shock, immediately looked out into the audience of six hundred. He then turned and quickly checked himself to see if anything was on fire. His silk shirt was incinerated around the waist, and his bright blue velvet jacket was blackened, but fortunately he suffered no burns. Unfazed, Paul drop-kicked the drum offstage and continued with his performance. But the toy soldier that had once stepped so smartly out of the door forever after looked as if it had taken a cannonball to the gut.

"Fire does what it does," Paul says. "You can utilize something one hundred times and the hundred and first time it will do something different than you expected. That happens every show."

Paul speculates that it is the "impermanence" of fire that attracts people, although some find the manipulation of fire physically threatening or intimidating. "Sometimes people come up to us afterwards and say our shows were frightening to them—like they were scared," he says. "I don't really know what to think about that. To me it's beautiful."

Douglas Berry, one of the newest members of the troupe, has this to offer: "I think everybody's attracted to fire. For thousands of years, generations upon generations of humans have wanted to hold it and control it. And you can't help it. When [we're] in a bar and light up a torch, everyone *has* to look. When you go camping, what do you do but sit around and look at a fire? It's ingrained in us."

After the evening's performance of "The Garden," Flam Chen moves *en masse* to a downtown bar, aptly named Vaudeville. It's located along a short, two-block strip that provides a haven for students of the nearby university.

I arrive early, while the members of Flam Chen are still changing out of their costumes, and am thus witness to the strange impression the group makes as they enter the bar around midnight.

They stagger in on stilts, white clown faces eerie in the darkness. For their after-show apparel, the men have favored plaid, thrift-store jackets and bowler hats, resembling sideshow barkers that have somehow gotten lost on their way to a nocturnal midway. The girls, Nadia and Geneva, are wearing loose, flowing pants and glittery bra tops. Geneva's hair is still in ornate braids from the performance; Nadia's, pulled back in a high ponytail behind her shaven front, recalls both a Buddhist monk and *I Dream of Jeannie*.

They are stepping over tables on their giant stilts, leaning over customers and creating delightful mayhem. Nadia, with no stilts, leaps nimbly on the bar; she kneels, arching her back so that her ponytail brushes the counter behind her, and dramatically lowers a small, lit torch into her open mouth. She extinguishes it, removes the torch and then inserts another.

All around the members of Flam Chen mimic her—first weaving torches over the enchanted bar patrons, then eating fire as if it were a delicious new food. Stilts are removed and the poi are lit. A classical guitarist seated on a small stage becomes part of the act, strumming faster as the balls of flame circle round and round.

I think of this scene the next day when Jess talks about the importance of audience interaction.

Before becoming involved with Flam Chen, he says, "My friend Matt and I got really frustrated going out to shows and seeing people just standing around. We . . . wanted people to participate. We had these ideas to make masks, take them to an event and pass them out . . . We thought people would be less likely to worry about what they looked like, or whether they were cool or not, if they were wearing these masks." The two began putting together some street performances. "The idea was to engage people in something that was taking place in their own space."

Jess is still wearing the vividly patterned red and white vintage coat he wore the night before, closely buttoned and topped with a bowler hat. He is a small-framed but big-eyed man, with an expressive face belonging to the era of silent film.

Making theater is in some ways the inversion of his previous work as a social activist. "I got tired of constantly reacting to things—it feels like you're in their game," he says. "I came to

this with an activist concept of doing something out of my own vision by traveling, performing and playing with people."

"I've worked with a lot of indigenous rights groups and have been impressed by [native] peoples' attempts to keep their cultures," he continues, "to not have their culture totally washed out by corporate, homogenized, American *stuff*—you know, junk food culture. We wanted to try to create some culture of our own, so that we would be out there on the streets, having festivals and times that we look forward to in the year, making festal culture happen. Celebrate."

Months later, Flam Chen arrives in my hometown of Dallas to play the last gig of their summer tour. All six members of the cast, plus Nadia's eight-year-old daughter, a cameraman and a hitchhiker from New Orleans, bunk down in a friend's concrete-floored studio while the tour bus undergoes repair. Their 1974 silver anniversary edition Crown Coach apparently has seen enough of the road for one year.

The tour has not been an easy one—if there has ever been such a thing as an easy road show. Their summer season kicked off at the New York Fringe Festival, where Flam Chen was to have been a featured act, although advance publicity proved to be minimal. About thirty people showed up on their first night, to fill an outdoor amphitheater easily capable of seating several hundred.

Flam Chen had brought an elaborate set consisting of several stories of scaffolding to support the aerial components of their show. After setting up, the park service belatedly informed them it could not stay on the stage overnight. The troupe members worked into the early morning hours after putting on the show to dissemble everything. And for the next six days they spent every day putting it back up again. "If we had only known we would have done 'Ms. Spider,' because that show only needs a table and a few chairs," says Paul ruefully.

More hassles ensued. The bus was directed by festival organizers to park overnight in a lot full of delivery trucks, all of which started up in unison every morning at 6 A.M., filling the fire performers' bus with noise and exhaust fumes. After a series of phone calls, the troupe managed to get a permit to park their bus at the amphitheater, and secured a radio interview that brought in notably improved crowds. But dealing with the bureaucracy drained their enthusiasm for the Fringe Fest: they were almost happy when the final night was rained out, giving them a chance to slip over into Brooklyn to do some high energy flame-throwing at a warehouse party.

The group next moved on to the Philadelphia Fringe Festival, where they performed in an alternative tent set up to house acts that weren't invited to be part of the "mainstream" fringe fest. Then the bus headed south, across the country towards New Orleans.

It was there, in the state of swamps and Spanish moss, that they met with actual tragedy. A fellow-performer and friend of the troupe, Lucas Cox, had been killed just days before their arrival. Lucas had been an enthusiastic supporter of Flam Chen for almost ten years, and was a particularly close friend of Paul. Lucas had actually been delivering flyers for Flam Chen's upcoming performance in New Orleans when his

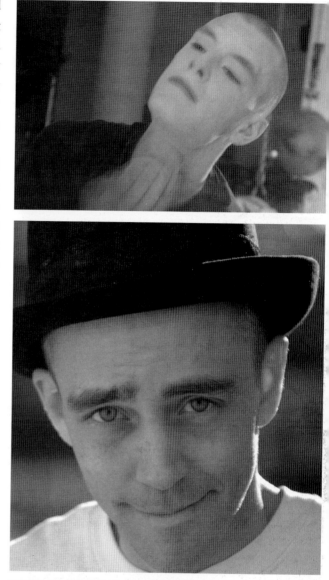

bicycle was struck by a car. Completely devastated by the news, Flam Chen arrived in time to attend their friend's memorial. It was held in a public park, with mourners forming a circle around a large tree.

The performance that night—a double-bill with the Know Nothing Family Zirkus—turned into another memorial of sorts. Freaks, street buskers and performers of every type turned up to see Flam Chen, Lucas' favorite group. "The only good thing about Lucas' death is that it allowed us to really see the effect he had on people here, how much he contributed to the community," Paul later says.

After that experience, the breakdown of their bus in Dallas is met with some resignation by the sobered troupe. Fortunately, they are able to borrow photographer Phil Hollenbeck's toy-covered art van (dubbed "The Chariot of Desire") to get to their gig at Club Clearview. This time they plan to present 'Ms. Spider,' a sort of wicked children's tale involving characters such as a fire-juggling rabbit and a lady spider who presses poisoned tea upon her would-be victims. Their costumes are a mixed assortment of shabby top-hats, tail-coats and corsets mixed with animal parts: horns, tails, ears. People passing the Chariot of Desire gawk at the wildly-decorated vehicle—and then do a double-take at the weird cast of anthropomorphic characters sitting behind its windshield. A city bus driver looks over and nearly falls out of her seat laughing.

The crowd this time is not the respectful theater crowd that attended the New York Fringe, with hands folded and mouths shut in anticipation of art. The club's denizens are young, drunk, college-aged kids who have come to thrash along to the music of headlining act "Bozo Porno Circus," a speed metal band whose show features girls doing a live S&M act. Having booked the troupe at the last minute, the club hasn't informed anyone about the fire dancers. Jess, dressed in a top hat with floppy rabbit ears and mask/snout, leaps onstage and attempts to scream his introduction conjuring the curious, Alice-in-Wonderland world of Ms. Spider. But the audience's conversational roar is louder. "Show us yer titties," a heckler yells.

Jess picks up a spotlight and beams its red light into the back of the room. A flame rises above the heads of the crowd in back, dancing upon the tip of a tattered umbrella. Bodies side-step to make way for Paul, a.k.a. "Mr. Polliwog" as he dances to the front in a tattered waist-coat and tails. Despite the humor of his approach and almost clownlike apparel, his silver-painted face looks fierce, particularly with a pair of horns emerging from his temples. One by one the other members of the group follow suit, and began displaying their skill with fire fans, canes, poi and other implements.

As they gambol about onstage, the newest member of the troupe makes an appearance: a female character with wicked, highly arched eyebrows wearing a long skirt and short black veil. Adeena Tomiyama was selected for the tour to replace Geneva, who left for graduate school in London. Adeena, a nineteen-year-old Japanese-American, is a small but potent addition to the troupe. She cackles and jabbers in a high-pitched, nonsensical squeal, while her lithe frame, clothed as Ms. Spider, leans and curls around the other characters, enticing them to a highly suspect cup of tea.

At 6'8", Douglas is the most visually arresting of the group, whether imposingly solemn in white kimono robes or—as tonight—playing a sort of goofball, with his lanky arms and legs hanging out of too-short overalls. He is the last to join the lineup on stage, where everyone else is busily demonstrating their exceptional fire prowess. In a great comic moment, he looks around, pulls out a cigarette lighter, and with an expression of dumb happiness, lights a flame of his own. It gets a laugh from the audience.

By now, the hyperactive Ms. Spider has assembled the rest of the characters in a row of chairs near her table. With an oozing smile she passes teacups around, becoming incensed when no one ventures to take a drink. Her wrath falls upon Douglas; she pounces on his back and begins hammering on him, a little angry tick on the back of a large beast. When she finally manages to wrench a small torch from his hands she begins torturing him: still clinging to his back she rakes the fiery torch across his bare chest. The other characters, anxious to get on her good side, come to her aid and help hold him down. First one arm, then another, she grabs and slowly draws fire along it. It's a cruel but also highly amusing spectacle: Douglas' terrified country bumpkin character can't seem to believe that a cute little spider girl can be so vicious.

For the finale of the show, all the characters get out their poi and spin fire, incredibly fast and close—both to each other and to the audience. Paul, eyes blazing out of his silver, horned face, is on the ground in front of the stage, spinning maniacally but with extreme concentration, his flaming wicks just inches from the crowd. A girl in the front row shouts, "Hey, will you light my cigarette?" Paul ignores her the first time. But as she attempts to shove her way into his space, whining about getting a light for her cigarette, Paul yells at her to shut up. "Why are you so angry?" she yells back. She continues heckling him—a rather dangerous activity—until all the performers gather on the stage again. There the magical animal-creatures drink flame out of delicate cups and saucers, and, while losing consciousness, are wrapped up neatly in Ms. Spider's web.

The bar audience gives them a loud ovation, and when Calvin, the group's martial arts specialist, lifts his shirt and shows his hairless chest to the "show-us-yer-titties" guy, the applause and cheers rise even louder.

"That wasn't even close to the toughest audience we've had," Paul says later.

Their bus readied, Flam Chen departs for the long drive home to Tucson. This year's Day of the Dead procession is only a few weeks away, and the group has much to do—puppets to make, workshops to hold, a new performance to rehearse. The Day of the Dead has become a focal event for the arts community of Tucson, bringing together all kinds of performers, artisans and children. While the event isn't Flam Chen's alone, it's not too much to say that they serve as the spark that ignites the rest of the event. It's the realization of the dream of many who, like Jess, share the aspiration to "make festal culture happen. Celebrate."

ENIGMA & FRIENDS @ BROS. GRIM SIDESHOWS

IT IS CLOSE to noon in a rented apartment in Seaside Heights, N.J., when The Enigma stumbles out of the bedroom wearing black shorts. Even half awake this modern-day legend looks imposing, with implanted horns rearing out of his skull and his entire body covered with intricate, blue, tattooed puzzle pieces. His right eye is nearly swollen shut on account of the tattoo work done on his eyelid yesterday; it looks like a painful bee sting. The horned blue vision manages a nod and a friendly smile before heading to the bathroom.

One of the most visually interesting performers currently working in the revived form of sideshow, Enigma, a longtime sword-swallower, has found his own appearance to be a double-edged sword. Unauthorized uses of his image have been so numerous that he no longer agrees to pose for pictures without compensation. He has been the unwitting (and of course, unpaid) model for a German advertising campaign, has served as the cover of a student's graduate thesis, and so on *ad infinitum*. Mostly he doesn't find out about such transgressions until, for example, someone calls from Europe and says, "Guess who I saw on a billboard over here?" Almost like a supermodel, Enigma's extraordinary appearance seems to lead some kind of larger, public life in the world of images than does his actual self—and to gaze upon him is to immediately be thrown into an age-old questioning about the relationship between the outer body and the inner soul. Friends in his adopted hometown of Austin, Texas are quick to assure that his ferocious exterior hides a very decent, kind human being. But one wonders whether the self-made freak ever feels trapped by his own extraordinariness.

A few minutes later, his wife Katzen walks in, looking like a tattooed, nineteenth century rendering of Puss-in-Boots. Her tiger-striped, tattooed face and cat whisker implants (actually cheek piercings with removable Teflon fibers) peer out coyly from underneath a swashbuckling, broad-brimmed hat. Her outfit is completed by a one-shouldered, red tank top; a full black skirt bustled with metal clips; and of course, boots. She tenderly administers to the

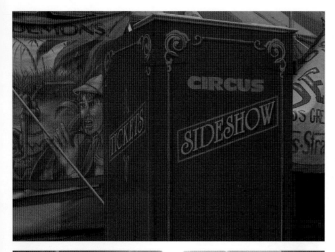

ailing Enigma with his swollen eye, moving back and forth between the kitchen and the bedroom with breakfast plates.

In the living room, cigarette in hand, sits Ken Harck, mastermind of the Brothers Grim Circus Sideshow. This Chicago-based purveyor to the public of freakish delights employs performers such as Enigma and Katzen to perform in an authentic recreation of a 1920s sideshow, an attraction he dreamed up after years of collecting circus posters and memorabilia. His catalog of over 4,000 original pieces of circus art and artifacts includes P.T. Barnum's personal tea service and china, vases given to Barnum by the Czar of Russia, and even a lock of hair from Barnum's baby book.

The 47-year-old carnie sis on a folding chair and takes a deep drag from his cigarette. His hair is wavy and blonde, his eyes a light blue. P.T. Barnum, he is saying, was the world's first advertising genius.

"He was a genius but he also had a reputation as a charlatan," Ken says. "In his show there was good and evil all mixed together. If you didn't like the two-headed baby you could look at the butterfly exhibit."

Ken is also an expert on circus music. "It's anything but corny. It's passionate, depth-y, and a lot of it was written in a minor key. It was creepy, goth-y, devastatingly cool. It should be there every time you do it." He pops a cassette tape of whistling calliope music into a player and turns it up—real loud.

"This is a great song," he yells. "This is called 'Officer of the Day.' You can almost hear the joy of a family spending an afternoon at the circus." The song comes to an end and Ken continues.

"People don't realize that the word 'tradition' means something so great you can't make it better," he says. "The thing about circus is that people way cooler than you or I came up with this two hundred years ago. If you bother to study them in the least what you get back is the mysteries of the world."

But Ken's performers aren't entirely traditional in the sense of having learned their skills on the midway from old-time performers. In the gap between the death of sideshow in the mid-eighties and its revival a decade later, these performers taught themselves sword-swallowing from books, fire-breathing from traveling around the country with anarchist performance troupes, and glass-eating on the stages of rock and roll clubs. The Bros. Grim Circus Sideshow is in fact a crossroads where the elite of the alternative, reinvented circus performers come to pay homage to the past. There is Danielle de Meaux, former ultravixen of the campy splatter-gore band GWAR and leader of her own Girly Freak Show; William Darkë, ex-leader of the William Darkë Psycho Circus & Freak Show; Camanda Galactica, former ringmistress of the tribal nomadic End of the World Cirkus; and, of course, Enigma and Katzen. Tyler Fyre, a young fire manipulator and escape artist, is perhaps the only exception, having honed his skills with performers at Coney Island where the last traditional sideshow in the U.S. remains in residence.

A few blocks away from the apartment, the sideshow's candy-striped tent is set up on the very edge of the boardwalk overlooking the Atlantic Ocean. Rain has slicked the grey boards so that they seem to match the sky, the ocean; there are only a few visitors milling around between the food concessions and gaming booths. I follow Katzen for a short distance along the boardwalk, observing the happy smiles and pointed fingers that accompany her passage, and which she doesn't appear to notice. The spectators don't display shock or trade furtive nudges as they might upon viewing someone else with extreme body modifications. They seem genuinely delighted, as if a Disney cartoon had decided to come to life and go for a stroll. Katzen is a big, walking, talking cat, and the general consensus is that she's cute. She slips through the canvas opening of the tent and soon the sound of an electric guitar tuning makes its way onto the almost empty boardwalk.

Unfortunately, bad weather has kept the boardwalk clean of visitors for most of the summer season. In addition to the financial hit, the onslaught of nature has included high winds that have torn down banners and threatened to knock the sideshow into the sea. Even with 6,000 pounds worth of giant concrete blocks anchoring the tent, the performers found themselves one night literally clinging to tent poles as they were lifted into the air by the wind. Then, on the Fourth of July, the power for the entire city of Seaside Heights was knocked out by a storm. Bros. Grim continued to put on its show by the light of flashlights, when Enigma, as part of his act, grabbed a chainsaw and started chasing a girl. Police patrolling the darkened boardwalk surrounded and handcuffed the horned monster until Ken caught up and hastily explained, "It's OK, it's his job. Just like you arrest people, it's his job to chase people with a chainsaw." Since then, inclement weather has kept most of their audience away.

Time for a change of scenery.

* * *

An aromatic smell of fresh sawdust carried on warm evening air rises from the floor inside the pink and green-striped tent, which glows within from a single string of bare lightbulbs. To the front: a raised stage. To the rear: the Museum of Ancient Ritual, Oddities and Witchcraft, a collection of monkey-tooth necklaces and fetuses in jars typical of old sideshows. Outside, in the Texas countryside, an assortment of howls belonging to the neighboring haunted house fills the autumn air. And directly in front of the Bros. Grim Circus Sideshow, a man on a platform delivers his pitch.

"Hey now look here, hey now look here." Ken, in a button-down white shirt, drones into his microphone like a practiced salesman. "Look at these pictorials . . . These freaks, these oddities, these marvels—they are all alive and here tonight. Alive on the inside. They present themselves undraped, unashamed, before your very eyes."

The banner line is up—a double row of canvas paintings depicting such dubious wonders as the "Wolf Boy," "Spidora" and "Monsters of the Deep." Ken maneuvers the crowd expertly during his "bally," a sideshow term for the pre-show pitch. Camanda, balancing a heavy python snake around her neck like a feather boa, ascends the steep ladder to the bally stage.

"Camanda Galactica and her Dance of Death," Ken says to a growing assembly. "This lovely young lady is going to defy death tonight, before your very eyes, as she performs with this ten-foot-long Amazonian python. She's gonna twitch it; she's gonna twatch it—and you're all going to get to watch. Now I want you to see Camanda and her Dance of Death; I want you to see Katzen the Tiger Lady risk one of her nine lives; and I want you to see the Anatomical Wonder, William Darkë . . ."

Spectators begin moving towards the ticket booth, which is built unnaturally high, in authentic form, to encourage ticket buyers to leave their change on the counter as the crowd presses from behind. A vintage 1923 calliope, attached to a generator, kicks into action and begins churning out a loud whistling tune. The crowd moves under the canvas flaps and into the open sawdust-covered oval where the lights are beginning to go down. Ken's amplified voice is barely audible outside over the calliope.

"The money you spend you will never remember; the things you see you will never forget!"

What follows is so fast-paced and electric that spectators barely have a moment to laugh or gasp between consecutive astonishments. The blue figure of Enigma, wearing a gold robe and turban, hits the spotlight first.

"Ladies and gentleman, behind you is the Theater of Death. Before you, the Theater of Life. What does this mean?" He looks about imposingly, then suddenly picks up speed. "It means there's no TV, no remote control, everything you see here is live so put your hands in the air and bring them together for that Anatomical Wonder, Mr. William Darkë!"

William does fire-eating and fire trans-fers, dragging the tips of flaming brands along his bare arms, then finishing with a giant fire spit as the Human Volcano. Enigma returns to the stage and chops a cucumber off of Katzen's neck with an axe, and with the briefest build-up possible ("And now—sword-swallowing!") drops to one knee and lets a 24-inch blade sink all the way down his gullet till the pommel rests on his lips. He cracks a few jokes and then Camanda takes the stage, placing her pliant body across a bed of nails. William returns and does a crowd-pleasing contact juggling number with crystal balls. Camanda runs around to a velvet-draped box, sticks her head through a mirrored opening and becomes "Spidora," a glass-crunching half-woman half-spider. Tyler Fyre does the Human Blockhead, tapping nails, screwdrivers and running power tools into his nose.

Katzen slinks onstage next dressed as a sequined showgirl—and proceeds to work a corsage pin through her upper eyelid and brow. A brunette girl in the audience stiffens and keels over backwards, into the soft sawdust.

Enigma returns to perform "the most dangerous stunt ever performed on stage—balloon animal tricks!" He pulls out a condom, huffs the condom up his nose, then reaches back into his throat and pulls it out of his mouth. The audience groans and screams and laughs—and all the more so when Enigma reverses the process, causing the slime-covered condom to go back in his mouth and pop out of his left nostril to wave at the crowd. There is a big, fiery finale with

Enigma and Katzen on their guitars, and then the lights come up. Camanda and William are already on the outside stage assisting Ken with his next bally as the first audience leaves. This circular process of bally and stage performance will repeat itself five or six times in a night, with no breaks for the performers.

Next day, on the grounds of the haunted house, the pink and green tent is blaring Metallica's "Black Album" as theme park employees began showing up for their nightly shift. Dylan, the 24-year-old sound technician and the most junior member of the sideshow, is at the controls. "When the others aren't here, *I'm* in charge," he says, turning up the volume just a hairsbreadth more. He is wearing black shades and a black T-shirt that says "Cat—The Other White Meat."

Through a side flap in the tent, the performers arrive to begin preparations for the evening's performance. Danielle, with short blonde hair and glittery purple and green eyeshadow, is as intense as a live wire. She seems to have absorbed all the energy of the 170,000 volts that the Tesla coil is capable of sending through her.

"I built my first Tesla coil when I was in the fourth grade," she says. "I've shot ten-, twelve-foot lightening out of my hands. The electricity feels like your whole body is falling asleep or like getting tattooed all over. Once I had a wig catch on fire. I am the female Evil Knieval!"

Previously she was made famous by her role as Slymenstra Hymen, the nasty female member of GWAR. "I made myself something I wasn't because I wanted to be onstage," she says. "But I got sick of rock and roll clubs. Creating Girly Freak Show was a liberation for me. We had a slew of girls, a rotating cast from all types of variety acts: Kitten on the Keys, Camanda Galactica, Ula the Painproof Rubber Girl. I felt like I was gonna die it was so much fun."

Today she's only collecting her gear, though, as she has another gig out west and Camanda is taking over her particular slot in the show.

Camanda, a long-legged beauty, is sitting on a trunk drawing harsh black lines on her face with makeup. The sideshow is still a relatively new place for her, after years of performing with a more nomadic group, the End of the World Cirkus, for whom circus was more inspiration than literal realization

"I call what we did 'creative survivalism,'" she says. "We had this traveling entity of kids using art both as a survival mechanism and to plant seeds of subversion . . . But it couldn't last forever. When I was invited to work here it really opened my eyes to new possibilities of performance, with sideshow."

Camanda once ended up in the hospital after trying to learn sword-swallowing. "I didn't know it but I had strep throat at the time and it abscessed. I was ready to chill out after that." Now she sticks to "safer" activities like eating glass and the bed of nails.

Enigma shows up backstage looking monochromatic: blue baseball cap, blue metallic loops in his ears, shorts painted with blue puzzle pieces. The soles of his feet are the only part of him that is not blue. Even his light blue eyes coordinate with his skin.

Enigma began his famous metamorphosis while performing as Slug the Sword-Swallower in the earliest incarnation of the Jim Rose Circus Sideshow.

"It was quite a time back in '91," he recalls. "When I hooked up with Jim I also hooked up with the Torture King, the Amazing Mister Lifto and a gentleman named Matt 'The Tube' Crowley. It was a very magical time, because in one weekend we all came together in Seattle to suddenly be this troupe, this amazing group of highly creative minds who had been working in their closets doing this stuff.

"Before that I never thought about more than swallowing swords, how amazing and cool that was. To suddenly meet others that were pushing the same boundaries was very inspiring. So I thought, 'What more could I do?' I could swallow swords, I could eat fire, I could eat glass. That's kind of like the inanimate thing. I could also do an animate thing, I could devour animate things. I called up the Torture King and said, 'Hey, I'm going to eat a slug.' And he was totally horrified so I knew that I had a decent act."

At the same time, Enigma, who only had a single tattoo on his left arm, began envisioning a full-body theme for himself. " I was thinking I could be all plaid or paisley or anything," he says. "But I came up with the puzzle idea, just thinking of wallpaper pretty much. I talked to some tattoo artists about doing it and they all kind of laughed at me. And I talked to people about getting my own equipment to do it because I thought it might be tough to do some of those intimate areas."

But it was not until the 1992 Lollapalooza tour that he met someone willing to help him implement the design: a seventeen-year-old girl with a strange fantasy of her own and no professional tattoo experience.

"I was sitting around in a coffee shop in Atlanta, Ga. with the Torture King and a gentleman called Carey Thornley (if you're into conspiracies a-go-go, you'll know that Carey Thornley is the guy who was writing a biography on Lee Harvey Oswald). And while Torture King was in this in-depth conversation, I was sitting there, being the young kid that I was, just gynoscoping. And I noticed these two ladies sitting at the table across from me. I threw a quarter in my eyeball and got a little applause, so I walked over there and said 'Mind if I sit down?' I talked to Katzen, who said she was also an entertainer."

Katzen, a juggling street performer and visual artist, found herself hanging out on the tour bus at Lollapalooza the next day. "He was interesting," she recalls. "The conversation we had that day was about a four hour-long philosophical conversation. We just went everywhere, it was fun . . . and it was really funny because he had invited another girl on the bus too, and I got the feeling 'He's trying to see which one impresses him more, to see which girl he's going to hang out with' kind of thing. I thought he was a bit of a player or something. But we really hit it off and that's when we started talking about the tattooing."

"I've always had very vivid dreams and sometimes I can remember them really well," Katzen continues. "As a child I had this one dream that I felt *great* in. It was kind of like a flight dream, where everything feels light and wonderful. Except I was surrounded by this landscape where

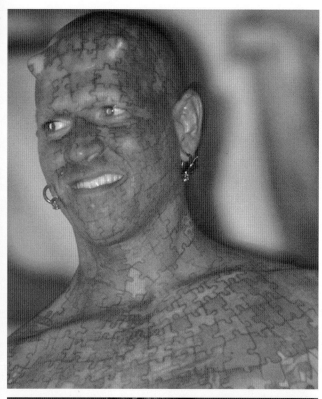

the ground was all purple and the sky was all green. And I saw myself with stripes like this and it just seemed like a fantastic world that I could somehow touch. It was really palpable.

"So I started drawing pictures of myself with the stripes on me. One of my earliest self-portraits that I still have was when I was nine years old and was asked in art class to do a boring self-portrait exactly as I would be in reality against a brick wall. I did it, but one part of the brick wall was pulling away and there was this luminous purple jungle behind it; and where the brick wall came across my face, where the breakaway part was, I had those stripes on my face. That was my nine-year-old portrait. I ended up getting an A on the portrait even though the teacher was like 'I really shouldn't give this to you because you were supposed to do it just like in reality.' I saw myself like that but I never thought I would actually do it. It was really meeting up with someone else who wanted to be completely tattooed. I was like, well, if I can do this and help him along the way, then I can make a dream come true."

At the artist's collective where she lived in Atlanta, Katzen had only recently begun tattooing friends by hand using an adapted Japanese method. Her first tools were paintbrushes with needles sewn on with dental floss and then coated with candle wax to keep them from slipping. But she felt she already had a good understanding of the technique. Before leaving town, Enigma gave her one of his swords and promised to send her money for tattooing equipment and a plane ticket.

"Everybody in the troupe was like, 'You're going to send this woman money? You're never going to see that money again! I can't believe you're trusting her!'" Katzen says. "So he was fighting everybody's voices to hear his own, to make it happen."

In January of the following year, Enigma took a month off from touring with Jim Rose and sent for Katzen, who then completely outlined all the puzzle pieces covering his head and body during a marathon six-week tattoo sitting. The morning of his debut performance as The Enigma was spent from one to seven a.m. finishing the lines on his skull. The same day, February third, he drove all the way to Portland to perform at the Roseland Theater in front of a camera crew who had already received publicity photos showing the partially obscured face of The Enigma. "I had told everybody in the troupe that I was going to do this, but they totally thought I was joking," says Enigma. "Nowadays they all laugh when I say that I'm going to do something but they know it's going to happen."

"At the time I was doing Enigma's tattoos we also conceived our daughter, Caitlin, and I wasn't able to start on my own tattoos until after I had her," said Katzen. "So I waited. She was about three months premature; they said it was because I had been walking around all day. I'm not one to pay attention to that kind of stuff. I have lapses of time—I mean, I'm just not concerned with it at times. I think a lot of artists are that way. So anyway, I had her and the week after having her I started tattooing myself. I did most of my legs myself, from my knee to my ankle, and I outlined my whole left arm. I had somebody else do my right arm. I started making needles for a local tattoo shop. They wouldn't give me a job, but they said that if I came by and made needles they would tattoo me. So that's where I got my backpiece started."

Her most painful tattoo, she says, was on her lower eyelids. "I was on the floor of the New York City Tattoo Convention, on a raised table, and a woman was tattooing me under the eyes and we had bodyguards on each side of the table because people were walking right by. It was a very visual experience for everyone—it's like 'whoa, there's a person getting their eyelids tattooed right in front of us.' The BBC just happened to be there at the convention; they conducted the interview *while* I was getting my eyelids tattooed."

Enigma, on the other hand, underwent successive surgeries to have increasingly larger Teflon horns implanted in his head. Which begs the question: Why?

"In school you learn that you're gonna work for fifty years, maybe get married, have kids that scream at you, a wife that yells at you, and then die. That's kind of serious. That's some serious shit to lay on a kid," says Enigma. "Especially one that's lived most of his life in the fantasy books that he read and the TV shows that he watched like *Incredible Hulk* or *Twilight Zone* or *Battlestar Galactica*. I lived most of my life in the comic books, even though I was mostly in the back seat of a car going back and forth to private lessons. [He took ballet, tap, flute and singing as a child to gain "an appreciation of the arts."] My laws were the laws of comic books and fantasies, not the laws of corporate business and getting ahead.

"So, you have to reinvent everything. You have to all of a sudden understand creation—'Oh yeah, I *am* that.' You have to understand creation on its basic level. You have to go all the way back to square one and redefine all the physical principles around you. I did that at quite a late time in my life.

"This is who I am. It's funny. You get a tattoo and it is on your physical being, but it is also, since you cannot separate the mental and the physical—they are one and the same—it is who you are mentally as well. People forget that. So when I say I am The Enigma, you may look at my skin and go oh well, he's just a guy with blue skin. But I am The Enigma in my head as well. When you put any kind of marks on your body or pierce your nose or whatever, you're also putting a piercing in your brain."

Enigma has a standard joke about his mother's attitude towards his line of work. "If I was president of the United States, mom would call and say 'Are you eating your greens?' And if I was a cab driver she'd say 'You're gonna kill yourself in that cab someday.' You can never be good enough for mom." Being featured in National Geographic several times, traveling around the globe and being tattooed by over two hundred artists worldwide gives normal-world credence to his chosen profession. But, Enigma adds, "You know she's never seen me perform and probably never will." He laughs. "She doesn't appreciate 'the artistic integrity of the piece.' She's just not able to . . . it's too much for her."

But his now ten-year-old daughter, who resides with her grandparents, has a different opinion. "She thinks its great!" says Enigma. "She's fascinated by it and loves us very much. And who knows, maybe she'll major in contractual law later on and help us with our stuff. Hopefully she'll understand the lack of immediacy and—"he grins—"understand that we're trying to build an empire and take over the world."

"I started from the standpoint of doing it for myself, to make a dream happen," says Katzen. "If you are as much *you* as you can be, and the world can't accept you or deal with you, then what is the world good for? Really, that was my philosophy. I have to be happy with myself and hopefully the world will enjoy what I did. That's all you can do. I think it's great to expand people's minds just by showing up in a room. You never really foresee what your life is going to be like, but I'm pretty happy with where I've been, what I've seen, what I've done. I think it saved me from a life of crime."

After eight years with Jim Rose, Enigma and Katzen have started their own business marketing themselves as the Human Marvels. At first they traveled with their own show, the Puzzillion; now they are concentrating on writing music and learning to handle their new guitars. While playing songs about sideshow arcana, the odd couple performs old and new stunts, including the "gavage": an unholy utilization of a medical gastric lavage unit that allows Enigma to drink a large quantity of liquid—any liquid—through the nose.

"Yeah, he has a tube running up his nose while he's doing a guitar lick," says Katzen. "Granted, music has always been a part of circus and sideshow, but what we're trying to do is intermingle it in a way that other people haven't."

She has already heard about the woman fainting during the show the previous night. "It's not my first 'falling ovation' but I love it when they happen," she says. "We've had people pass out when Enigma does the tube act. What we do is extreme for some people."

By the time the interview is over, darkness has fallen and the pink and green tent is once again glowing with electrical light. Seen from behind, the supporting beams of the stage form natural partitions, dividing the area underneath the stage into miniscule dressing rooms. The Tiger Lady ducks into her dressing cubicle and emerges with a veil around her face. Out in the sawdust ring, Ken is having a smoke before beginning the first bally of the night. Dylan, the youthful sound tech, is now walking around with a six-inch nail up his nose. The other performers, particularly the Human Blockhead, fondly regard the ingénue's efforts.

Ken is trying to get the "Wolf Boy" of Mexico across the border and into the U.S. in time to join his show. It's always a difficult proposition, he says, as the performer in question, Manuel Diaz, lives in a remote village with a single phone and no one who speaks English. Many members of Diaz's extended family have hypertrichosis, a condition of excessive hair growth on the face. [Manuel Diaz died November 7, 2003.]

Sideshows in the past always featured two kinds of "freaks": self-made freaks with peculiar talents (such as eating fire) and those born with actual physical abnormalities. True to its mission of historical reproduction, Bros. Grim tries to include both types. According to Ken, the sideshow lifestyle offers the latter group a number of benefits overlooked by the public.

"Historically, most sideshow freaks have always made a very good living and they were very proud of working on the shows," he says. "They basically feel they're going to be looked at anyway; this way they're turning their disfigurement or deformity

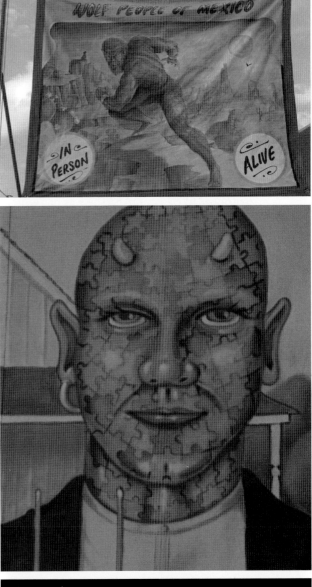

into something that actually makes money for them. The sideshow becomes their extended family." In the hierarchy of sideshows past, they were the highest, the royalty, of entertainers.

But as both traveling shows and the performers themselves aged, in the last half of the twentieth century, the sideshow inevitably lost some of its pizzazz. "It wasn't as glamorous as this is," says Ken, waving a hand around his gaudily striped tent. "And really the way to present these people is in an upscale way, so that they feel good about themselves performing."

"Our fat lady that we normally bring with us, she lives in a ghetto, she's going blind, she can barely make her rent each month. She's religious and she's got a little dog. When she's on our show, she talks about God and tells everybody that God loves you, and all the kids come up and pet her dog. At the end of her first day on the show, she was bawling, tears were coming out of her like a river. And she was hugging me so hard I could hardly breathe and telling me 'I didn't know that life could be this beautiful.' She was so excited and she thoroughly enjoyed being a performer. Those are the things that the public doesn't realize."

Ken puts out his cigarette on the ground and glances outside, where people are milling in front of the stage with their paper Coca-Cola cups, looking up at the banner paintings. "Nobody told me you'd have to re-educate people as far as the mooks or normals are concerned," he says. "You can show them a bally, bring out all the performers, tell them exactly what they are going to see inside and more often than not some woman with four kids will walk up and ask, 'What kind of ride is this?' You really are singing for your supper when you do this."

The performers are now gathered just inside the entrance to the tent. Camanda has hefted the heavy python onto her slender shoulders; William Darkë is holding his crystal balls; and Katzen is looking mysterious with only her feline eyes showing over the top of her sheer black veil. Enigma, who a moment before was flashing a movie-star white smile, is now holding three swords and deliberately putting on a more menacing aspect.

There's something about this moment that is like being on the tip of a rollercoaster before it goes down; something about the way the performers know that from here on out they are committed to a countless cycle of bally, laughter, screams, applause, bows and bally again, until the very last $5 bill possible is extracted from the crowd. Outside, the mooks, the rubes and the norms are waiting.

The freaks rush the stage to meet them.

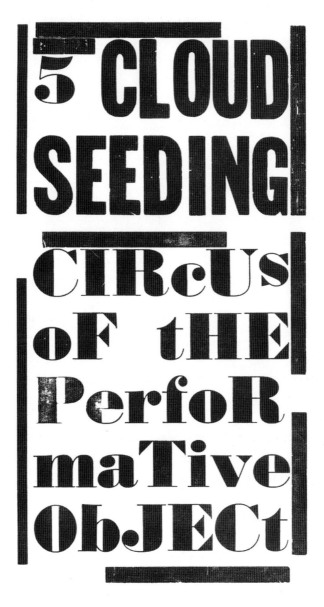

5 CLOUD SEEDING

CIRcUs oF tHE PerfoR maTive ObJECt

THE ELEPHANT FLUTTERED delicately in the night breeze as it hovered above the path of an abandoned railroad track. Forty-eight layers of architectural blueprint paper horizontally suspended by string composed its huge, yet almost incorporeal, body, woven through with tiny electrical lights. Four human bearers were required to hoist the frame, plus one to push a generator behind it. In the darkness, the nine-foot-tall, sixteen-foot-long creature began its stately approach.

From the platform of an old train depot next to the former tracks, a group of people stood waiting, aware that something was about to happen. There was an art exhibit inside, and on this, the opening night, they had already spent some time gawking at various paintings and sculptures, as well as helping themselves to hot apple cider. At a designated time, the crowd had been asked to step outside.

At a distance, the Object was simply a golden blur. Strains of accordion music, a single white light like the headlight of a locomotive. As it came closer, and the flashlight-bearing accordion player came into view, the audience gradually made out the trunk, the giant flapping ears and the shambling body whose paper layers shuddered realistically with each step like the giant corpus of a real elephant. Out of the night—an elephant, improbably composed, lit with fairy light. It majestically passed the loading dock and began to move off into the night.

Cheers and clapping broke out on the platform. With expressions ranging from childlike glee to hypnotized entrancement, people jumped down and gathered behind the elephant, clearly expecting a parade. For a while, the south Florida summer night was filled with the sounds of scuffling gravel, accordion notes and laughter as an impromptu procession took place, all eyes trained forward upon the papery, mythological body of the elephant-leader.

It was all a surprise for the elephant's creator, George Ferrandi. "I loved the idea of people standing at the depot waiting for something to pass by," she said. "I didn't expect two things. First, everyone wanted to get behind it and walk somewhere. They wanted a parade to happen. And also it didn't occur to me that people would applaud. I'd never had anyone clap for my art before. It was completely addictive."

The event marked the birth of Cloudseeding: Circus of the Performative Object, an almost bizarrely surreal circus in which Objects were the stars rather than their human creators.

At the time of the warehouse performance, George (short for Georgina) was teaching sculpture and electronic intermedia at the University of Florida in Gainesville. The idea of a circus came from a daydream she had while sitting through a boring school committee meeting. "I imagined a woman in a pink tutu walking on a tightrope above everyone's heads," she says. "I road my bike home and told my friend John [Orth] and that was what led to our initial ideas."

The pair started talking to their friends, mostly visual artists, about a circus of "performative" Objects. George roped in two of her undergraduate students, Dave Herman and David "Scout" McQueen, to work on the circus in exchange for course credit (at least initially). The definition of the new Objects included creations that required some kind of human interaction in order to be seen in their best light; they were meant to be seen in a performing, rather than static, state.

But a further distinction was then made between "performing" and "performative". Explains George, "The word performative contains a reflexivity that involves the Object reflecting back on its own making."

"We didn't think of ourselves as having any real circus skills. "What we do by not actually having those skills is turn the act into a metaphor. It has to do with starting with the Object, letting activity come from the Object."

George, thirty-six, is the oldest of the group and both by personality and profession fulfills the role of mother/teacher to the Cloudseeding troupe. She has long, loosely curling brown hair, simian-bright eyes and a pair of sheep tattooed in the crook of her right elbow (placed exactly so that they line up with her eyes when she puts her head down on her arm for a nap). "It seemed that circus allowed for theater, sculpture, improvisation, all these different things," she continues. "Not to overuse the tent analogy, but it does allow for endless possibilities and that has always been the case, from the original horse shows until now. It just becomes an endless possibility for audience interaction—and as a definition [circus] still means circle."

After the creation of the elephant came the circus trailer and stage. For $200 the group purchased a flatbed trailer from a mobile home mover in California. They added a new axle and tires, and welded together a square box on top with a semi-circular stage that neatly folded out of one side. Red velvet curtains attached with Velcro across the back and around the foot of the stage. It was a magic box that could be opened anywhere—in parking lots, empty fields—like a materialized dream.

The Cloudseeding name drew from the group's attempt to legally acquire warehouse space as a workshop. "In Gainesville the zoning laws with regard to warehouse spaces are pretty curious in that they don't allow artist's studios," says George. "Not that it's enforced, but it's not within the zoning law to make a warehouse into an artist's studio. I thought it was crazy and I asked, well what *is* legal? So we looked at the list: metal fabrication, boat making, cloud-seeding . . . We thought this was really great that you could have a cloudseeding station but you couldn't have an artist's studio. We decided to call ourselves Cloudseeding Studios, and I think as a metaphor it really suits us. It's an optimistic gesture, but at the same time, for an outdoor project, it's kind of a dooming prophecy."

An early flyer ballyhoos the marvels contained within a two-hour Cloudseeding performance: "1000 Pine Knots, 750 Galvanized Bolts, 500 Hand-Drawn Tattoos, 41 Fascinating Characters, 12 Prerecorded Songs, 10 Peruvian Clown Heads, 4 Fleeting Romances, 3 Live Bears, 3 Dead But Not Forgotten Bears, 4 Plastic Lawn Chairs, 6 All-Pink Ensembles . . . "

But the list is only a modest indicator of the excruciating artistic detail inherent in the show. The 1000 Pine Knots were hand painted onto the trailer to create the illusion of wood. The 500 tattoos, based on the venerable designs of Sailor Jerry, were also hand drawn onto a "tattooed suit" worn by the Long Eared Rabbit.

"It was really incredible," recalls George of the making of the suit. "It was made from old bed sheets and really, really beautiful. It took six people sitting around stitching." The process "felt like something from another century, a family of makers."

More Objects started bursting forth. Jesse Arnold, a graduate student, crafted translucent, fiberglass horse leg sculptures to be used as stilts. Scout made cast-iron fingers attached to ten-foot poles with which he could work the sound and light board from a distance. For the touring show, he created a small box called the "World's Smallest Clown Museum." When opened and set on its side, the two halves each displayed two hand-cast latex clown faces. Their noses—unbeknownst to most outsiders—ran the light board.

Circus was as an opportunity to create art all the way down, from the ticket stubs to the costumes, from the "finks" (an old carnie term for souvenirs) to the suitcases in which the troupe carried their gear. Every little item that accompanied the circus had to be painted or in some way embellished. It was completely, deliriously, over-the-top.

"We called it *circus baroque*, our attention to detail," says Christy Gast, who played the wheelchair-bound Last Mermaid of Florida. "My favorite circus baroque Object was a vice grip dipped in red glitter. I tried to take pictures of things like that. That pork chop ended up very baroque too."

"That pork chop" was part of co-founder John Orth's act. Wearing the Tattooed Suit, as well as a giant rabbit head, John would take this three-foot-long piece of cardboard painted to resemble a cut of meat and bizarrely dance a little jig in front of the stage's red velvet curtains to music from a live victrola, all the while spinning the pork chop. It was supposed to be a simple visual piece of strangeness, but in time John became attached to his Object. He gave it glitter, then faux fur and finally fireworks. Its origin as a humble pork chop was almost obliterated in circus baroque, added to which was the punishment it took on the road. Says one

member of the troupe, "By the end of the tour it was so burned and battered that no one could tell what the hell it was."

Not a few people wondered what the hell Cloudseeding itself was. The circus unveiled an obscure, even surreal, world with little attempt to explain it. Like shamans, they formed a bridge between ordinary life and an alternate reality in which Objects were supreme, and reveled in their latent powers.

In fact, even offstage the Cloudseeding members have a way of talking about their Objects with an emphasis that almost causes one to *hear* a capital "O." You get the feeling it's not so much reverence for their own artwork as a way of disingenuously dismissing themselves as performers and investing the Objects with a near-sentient life of their own.

Mindy Seegal Abovitz, one of the last people to join the circus, summarizes succinctly, "There was no attempt to perform. Everything was there before the audience showed up. That was the point: the Objects were there and we were there [to animate them]."

Mindy was the only member to come from a formal theatrical background, "which is probably why the circus was so magnetic for me," she says, "because it had nothing to do with engaging the audience. That's how I felt when I first saw them. At points the performers could care less whether the audience was interested in what was going on or if their attention was being held in any way. They cared much more about the piece of art that they were toying with or taking apart and putting back together. The act itself was peripheral."

Cloudseeding committed numerous theatrical no-no's. They stood with their backs to the audience. They let pieces drone on monotonously. They presented the far-fetched, curiously beautiful Objects on the traveling, velvet-lined stage and left it up to others to decide if it was an actual wonder or an artistic fraud of the medicine show variety. A reviewer from *The Dallas Morning News* who saw Cloudseeding perform outside of a local art gallery derisively compared it to the sort of circus a couple of children might put on in their parents' living room.

But to others, the initiated, the Cloudseeding circus had an ineffable beauty as well as a truly compelling weirdness. To quote Hutton Webster (writing on the evolution of circus from the mystery performances of nomadic tribes), "Witnessing such performances often amounted to being initiated into the group and the 'show' was, in reality, an oral library which contained all the society's secret doctrines. It was a reference system available to members only."[1]

Watching Cloudseeding was like that: you either agreed fundamentally to be initiated into the codified, secret realm of Objects, or you didn't.

My first encounter with Cloudseeding was in a darkened warehouse district on the east side of Austin, Texas. It was so dark on that June night that we initially missed the sign for the circus and had to turn around and drive back. Cutting the headlights, my friend and I saw that the circus was already in progress in the midst of a parking lot. The red velvet box was unfolded, and people were crammed (where did they all come from?) onto the rows of red, blue and yellow benches.

A high-end, flute-like noise vacillated over the speaker system. On stage were two persons dressed in jump suits with helmets that covered their faces. Each staggered about on a pair of translucent horse legs, each sculpture buttressed by welded metal caging and lit from within by a lightbulb. Both performers were wearing microphones and amplifiers; and as they circled each other onstage, clinging to either end of a piece of chain, occasionally squatting on top of their strange sculptural extremities, the feedback noise increased or decreased accordingly. The industrial-looking helmets and sounds, coupled with the animorphic legs, resembled the ritual retelling by confused aliens of a first visit to planet Earth. Their dance was both deliberate and off-kilter, as if one of them might fall over at any moment.

"I never practiced onstage," Jesse, the stilts' creator, later says. "I didn't want to 'get better.' I liked to generate anxiety, tension, between the audience and the person onstage. The whole show maintained this question: 'Are things working the way they're supposed to?'"

Next up was George as "The Great Monkeena." In a dramatic red velvet gown, she plucked a few notes on a ukulele, seemingly unperturbed by the strange tapping sounds that filled the pauses in her music. The audience began to giggle here and there as the unexplained tapping continued. The Great Monkeena finally pulled at a string hidden in her voluminous skirt and the entire thing parted in half, almost like a second set of theater curtains, to reveal a pair of miniature legs dangling down between her two regular ones. The parasitic legs were clothed in the same red and white-striped stockings as George's regular legs, and were tapping on a metal stool that she had straddled. The audience, shocked, laughed. Then the strange duet continued, the Great Monkeena sending out a tuneless, wavering ditty into the hot Texas night

while her parasitic legs tapped along. Standing above her on the trailer's roof, a man dropped dead swans on the stage about her. The Great Monkeena tried to ignore their landing thuds, but it made the extra legs slightly skittish.

Image followed inexplicable image. The Long Eared Rabbit engaged in a prolonged struggle to drag the life-size fiberglass hindquarters of a horse across the stage by his ears. The Last Florida Mermaid was scooped up from her wheelchair and placed on a low trapeze swing where she performed her fishtailed acrobatics. Two men wearing dresses and lashed to either end of a table suspended between them tried to have tea as smashing crockery flew about. The Great Monkeena sang a haunting, repetitive song while stirring quantities of sugar into a glass of water, with the tinkling of the spoon becoming somehow part of her song, a message that remained as encrypted as Morse code.

Jesse brought out his board-breaking, Big Foot heavy metal tribute act. Using a robotic arm of his own design and making only chimpanzee noises, he pantomimed the story of a young monkey encountering both Big Foot and a futuristic Space Monkey. The act culminated in the launch of the robotic arm towards a standing Big Foot cutout, the center of which held a small plank of wood that would be punched and destroyed by the arm. The audience was invited to try on the robotic arm and enjoy smashing some wood themselves to the music of Iron Maiden. When Jesse first created the arm, the circus went through two hundred wood planks in two days.

Unfortunately, "most of the time the arm didn't work," Jesse admits. "It was part of the tragic failure of the circus. Everyone in the audience thought I'd orchestrated it but actually I was really frustrated."

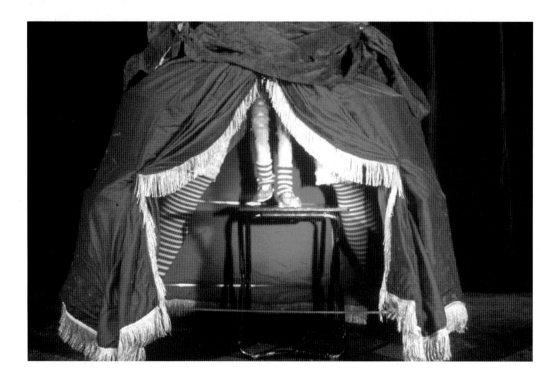

The tragic failure of Cloudseeding refers not so much to a literal failure (although, as with the arm, that occasionally happened too), but to an aesthetic that embraced vulnerability. The homely, the homemade, the sad . . . all of these had a place on stage, whether in the handmade suit or the bear whose face was constructed to fall off in a moment of pathos. When George describes Cloudseeding she says, "there's a tenderness about it that comes from something being broken and repaired; a tenderness that comes from a bruise."

Appropriately enough, George kept a record of everyone's injuries in her diary when they toured the country in 2001, honoring every smashed thumb and bruised knee with a place on the roster. Dave, meanwhile, symbolically painted a lightbulb on the inside of the trailer for every bulb that perished in the line of duty. Nothing, it seemed, was so humble that it was beyond either recognition or art.

The tragic perspective of the circus had its origin with both George and John, but its sense of nostalgia drew heavily from 27-year-old Dave Herman. He is a New York-based history buff whose outside projects have centered on the artistic recreation of lost spaces such as the dime museum and the old-fashioned barber shop. Circus, of course, fit neatly into his scheme. A debonair type, Dave favors bow ties and one of his five pairs of black and white wingtip shoes when not dressed down for work as a lowly art installer in Manhattan. Today we are holding interviews at his Williamsburg apartment in Brooklyn, sitting in a cool, basement level room which functions as his office. We balance on antique secretary chairs, surrounded by metal filing cabinets full of small, interesting objects (small "o") of the sort that artists often seem to keep around in case they prove inspiring or useful.

Dave is the show's talker. "I was the one who would engage the audience directly—'Come see freaks of all kinds, three-headed babies!'—and all that. I took the pressure off the other performers so they could work on their vignettes and not have to have a character that the audience had to relate to."

Dave was the one who found an old softcover book of circus lingo, its manilla pages listing words like "fink" and "flash" that the group incorporated into their show language. His wealth of historical trivia also came in good use when stalling in front of an audience, although at least once that knowledge went awry.

"We were in Lima, Ohio. It was a crowd at a street fair. This was one of our first shows; something went wrong backstage and I had to get out there and stall.

"So I wracked my brain to come up with something circus-y, and I thought of Coney Island and came up with the [true] story of Topsy the Elephant. But the Topsy story is a tragedy. Over the course of three years he killed three men, the last of which was his trainer, who fed him a lit cigarette and caused him to go on a stampede. They decided they needed to electrocute the elephant, so they called in Thomas Edison, who was living in New Jersey. At the time, Edison was trying to demonstrate the dangers of alternating current, and was going from animal shelter to animal shelter electrocuting the animals that were set to be euthanized in order to prove how deadly alternating current was. So he and his helpers set up these copper plates for the elephant to stand on, and they took all the electricity in Coney Island and piped it into

83

these bands that were around Topsy's legs. Edison had also just invented the motion picture camera, so the death was captured on film."

He shakes his head and laughs. "That was the wrong story to tell in a crunch situation. I learned that quickly by the blank faces on the parents and the tears in the children's eyes."

Dave recruited the next member of Cloudseeding, a Betty Page look-alike named Leslie Harding, who was a fellow student at New York's School of Visual Arts. Despite her pin-up glamorous looks—pale skin, black bangs, violet blue eyes—Leslie was too shy to go onstage.

Instead, she took charge of the fink stand, a pyramid of decorated suitcases to the side of the stage that displayed the group's handmade souvenirs. Interlaced with tiny, beaming Christmas lights, the surprising souvenirs were almost as entertaining as the show itself. Each member contributed something of their own making to the fink stand: Dave, the New York history buff, made Statue of Liberty name tags containing pieces of cloth rubbed on the statue (in the spirit of a religious icon); Mindy displayed a three-breasted bra; Christy sold mermaid fins and postcards of herself as the Last Florida Mermaid; Scout had latex clown masks and George offered posters that said "Go West Young Monkey."

"It had some of her beautiful characters on it," Leslie recalls of the poster. "George has this sensitivity that permeates everything. It was one of the things that made the circus so *beautiful*, and maybe not so hilarious or madcap. It became tender and sincere."

As for herself, Leslie sold the pack of tarot cards she created as her graduate thesis from the N.Y. School of Visual Arts, aptly titled "Super Duper Thesis-Style Tarot Cards." The cards contained her own drawings, and on the reverse side, poetry and diverse reflections from Omar Khayyam to Lou Andreas-Salomé.

"I wanted to create something that was of my own mind, but I didn't know what the hell was going on and I kept contradicting myself," Leslie says. "So I thought the tarot format was a great way to go. You pick one card and maybe the next card will contradict it, but it's all real."

Shuffling through the oversized deck, she selects the seven of Chelsea as an example. "Chelsea was my equivalent of pentacles, which is a money and tangible gain card," she explains. "It's not the most spiritual part of the deck. I called it Chelsea because, going to art school, that's where everybody wanted to be; and as artists everyone was kind of bitter that there was no treasure map, no step-by-step process that ended in a Chelsea gallery." The seven of Chelsea recounts a strange story about a mentally afflicted girl in Leslie's junior high band class who thought she was a unicorn.

Mindy Abovitz decided to audition for Cloudseeding after seeing a hometown performance in Gainesville. Initially her attempts to join were rebuffed; or rather, she got a low-key invitation to help assist the group in distributing flyers. But her desire to perform persisted and so, months later, she was finally asked to bring a proposal to a regular meeting of the circus. She brought her performance proposal—a velvet-lined, lighted box containing a caged feather—to the meeting and waited through four hours of business talk until, at 11 P.M., the new member agenda item was reached. Mindy introduced her box and showed a self-made video;

by the time other Cloudseeding members started jokingly querying her about her favorite movies and sexual orientation, she figured she was in.

"As the newcomer I did have to hang the curtains and do all the dirty work, the grunt work," she acknowledges. "I loved it. I did it all with joy. I was so blown away by the aesthetic. I really wanted to know how so many people could work together to create something . . . that looked like one person's idea."

Her burlesque act, as a three-breasted Jewish temptress doing a white-plumed feather fan dance, was a comedic hit.

"I was always interested in burlesque," says Mindy, who was raised in an orthodox Jewish home and speaks Hebrew. "That's what sexuality is like for me anyway—it's humorous and gaudy. I knew I wanted to do something like that and the circus was lacking sex.

"Bringing all of your artwork into a space that's devoid, a place like a parking lot where we traditionally played, and bringing people to it . . . is appreciated," she adds. "There's nothing comparable. People *really* appreciate it. And then you leave and they have only a memory of it. We rarely stayed in one place for more than a day."

Cloudseeding went on the road for six weeks at a time, the most that any individual performer could spare from his or her day job. Dave gained notoriety for using the tour as a pretext to steer the group to out-of-the-way historical monuments, although Christy, the only one with insurance, was the designated driver most of the time.

Christy had honed her performance skills earlier in Berlin, while living in a squat and busking with an all-female street ensemble, The Hausfraus. She was more than happy to take over the wheel for Cloudseeding. "I liked driving," Christy says. "I like getting to a city and meeting the people who are involved in their arts community—the people who have alternative spaces and live in the warehouse complexes—and sort of figuring out what every city's about." The only thing she didn't care for was the van's soundtrack. "Somehow we thought that we would have a CD player but we only had a tape player and the only tape we had was Modest Mouse. We had to listen to Modest Mouse over and over and over."

In New York City, three out of the six giant bears made by Cloudseeding got picked up and crushed by New York Sanitation after staff in a hotel mistakenly took the group's boxes, left in a basement storage area, for garbage. In Atlanta, several of the performers were hijacked by an experimental filmmaker who made them wear black robes and caper about on his set for four hours (a copy of the film shows them as a few indistinct blurs in the film's overall abstract treatment). In between, they made finks, performed with the Objects and blessed the existence of duct tape at the end of each show.

A small blackboard on the back of the trailer announced each upcoming destination, with the invitation to "Follow us to..." And in traditional circus fashion, the board was painted with the destination "China" after the last show, as the group headed back to Gainesville. "I don't know why they used to do that—I guess because home seemed so far away," says George. "It was such an insider, secret thing, being part of something that had its own language. There were some other terms we appropriated. We always talked about 'flashing out' the trailer rather than 'decorating.' And we talked about not wanting to be a 'fireball.'"

In times past, a fireball outfit was a show with a poor performance that allowed so many dishonest practices on its grounds that the towns played by it were literally burned up for any show that tried to follow it. "We were actually fireballed in New Orleans," George recalls. "Some people who lived in New Orleans at the time told us that they had heard about our show but didn't go because there were so many punk rock, crap circuses around then. They just assumed we were another one of them. I think there were eight people at that show, and that might have included the kids from the neighborhood that we let crawl in under the tarp."

Cloudseeding: Circus of the Performative Object has vanished from public view like the magic box that stood the night before in a now-empty field. Members began moving to the west coast and to New York City, in search of larger artistic horizons, in 2002. They reunited for a fall show at The Kitchen in NYC, but when they chose not to get together for a summer tour the following year, the circus was implicitly over.

"It's hard to get a bunch of independent artists together to work on something that belongs to no one," observes Dave. "I mean, nobody could really incorporate the circus into their own portfolio. Ultimately there were more people living separately than together, and all following their own lines of interest."

On a summer night, the Cloudseeding members are gathered on the roof of Dave's Williamsburg apartment building to bid a final, formal farewell to the circus. Slides from past performances are being projected upon a neighbor's brick wall while Scout grills salmon.

Chairs are drawn into a circle and tributes are paid (and stories told) about the members not present—John Orth, Alan Calpe, Will Heath and Brody Condon. George pulls out her journal and reads the list of physical injuries from past tours. Dave narrates a ballad in tribute to "Wagon Train"—an act he used to do that involved galloping across the stage on a plastic chair turned backwards. One day, exactly halfway through a show, his plastic steed bucked for the last time, shattered on the ground and sent a plastic shard into Dave's forehead. The story is pretty funny when told in rhyming couplets, particularly with a few beers at hand.

And they wax nostalgic.

"It remains my most amazing accomplishment," says George. "It's the most beautiful thing, knowing that there's no reason that this should have worked. None of us had any performance experience. We built this trailer even though we didn't know anything about building or towing requirements. All of these things that shouldn't have worked and yet maybe in spite of those things, or because of those things, we managed to do the show across the country for three different tours and people loved it. It just gives credence to that old adage that if you believe it you can make it happen."

"The biggest thing for me is that it happened at all, overriding all my cynicism," says Scout. "I remember on our second tour, we were going to Kalamazoo, Michigan. As we were loading up and heading out we could not get the weight distributed; the trailer started fishtailing after a block. So we unpacked and repacked three times. We did this for eight hours, until six in the morning.

"Finally we found someone who showed us how to lift the hitch and balance the trailer. Then it was a nonstop haul for twenty hours from Florida to Kalamazoo. When we got there, the students at the school where we were performing had written all over the place in chalk, there was a huge welcome for us. The energy there validated everything. That's one of my best memories."

The experience of the circus has changed the way the Cloudseeding members now pursue their own art. George's realization is typical:

"I went to a [university] program that really frowned upon collaboration," she says. "They were just more interested in a singular person's vision. I now have a whole new way of understanding what's possible for collaboration. I think it's fair to say a big part of the visual sensibility of the circus came from John Orth and myself. But it became an organism with its own aesthetic, and so all of us knew, 'oh yeah, that's circus' or 'that's not really circus.' It kind of established its own criteria and I think that's an interesting paradigm to work from creatively."

Says Jesse, "Some people say [collaboration] is avoiding responsibility. But I've always thought the strength of the collaborative is that you can totally reinvent yourself. I almost do it to get away from me."

George currently restores religious statues for churches when not working on her own artwork. Jesse makes robotic sculptures—infinitely more refined than the Big Foot smashing arm—that look like hypersterilized, Platonic forms of robots, very suitable for gallery exhibition. Christy, the Last Florida Mermaid, is working on inflatable sculptures inspired by rocks. When in Manhattan, she inhabits a tiny Greenwich Village apartment with a giant antique harp in it, both on loan from Baby Dee, a former member of the Bindlestiff Family Cirkus. Scout, now living with George, is exploring both kinetic sculpture and politically-motivated print work.

And somewhere in Gainesville, Florida, a painted trailer stands forsaken in a parking lot behind a local hospital. The roof, according to eyewitnesses, has sprung a leak. Inside, in the interior darkness, the Objects wait: a giant bear, a tattooed suit, six prosthetic arms, a horse's hindquarters. Having once been given sentience by the performative circus, do they remain . . . aware? And do drops of water, oozing in from the deteriorating rooftop, slide down the bear's cheeks to form . . . real tears?

———⟫●⟪———

1. Hutton Webster, Primitive Secret Societies: A Study in Early Politics and Religion, as quoted in Taylor, p. 119.

PARADOX IS PLACING purple orchids in his ears. Moondoggy is pulling red fishnet hose over his face, having stuffed the legs with balloons to form a hat with giant, waving tendrils. Meanwhile Philippe, over in a corner of the luscious park that surrounds San Francisco's Palace of Fine Arts, has shucked off his clothing, and is briefly naked as a newly laid egg before throwing a belt of fake animal pelts around his waist. Animal skins go around both legs, then a whole bag's worth of tribal jewelry goes around his neck. Brushing grey playa dust off from last week's campout at Burning Man, he methodically continues to wrap skins, feather boas and scraps of material around his arms.

It's a voodoo approach to costuming.

"Have you ever seen a Santeria altar?" asks Philippe, a lanky, longhaired Canadian. "It's all these different elements just piled on, sort of like this. The costume's never finished; I just keep adding things. It's the layering and mixing of elements that make it work."

The same might easily be said of Bantu Mystic Family Circus, a diverse 300-member troupe that draws inspiration from a gamut of world cultures to perform transformative, ritual circus theater.

The Bantu call themselves a nomadic magic healing arts circus whose ambitious goal is to combine "all art forms of all cultures, ancient and new, to share collective awareness . . . [to] gather and retell stories and songs, marry science and magic, and plant peace poles in [our] wake."

The idealistic Family members, mostly in their twenties and thirties, together own a jumble of skills suitable for the most eclectic of altars. Jugglers, temple dancers, capoeira warriors, DJ sound poets, tai chi sages, stilt walkers and aerialists are all part of this mix. They groove together like a custom-blend CD made by some impossibly cool DJ friend encompassing the height, width and breadth of every imaginable musical genre. And apparently no one

who wants to perform with the group has ever been turned away.

Says Moondoggy, "We're the most permeable membrane in show business."

"Anyone who thinks they're part of Mystic Family Circus probably is," says another.

As more Bantu members arrive in the park, their presence begins to cause a stir. Two stiltwalkers, Natalia and Dalamah, take to the air in their shimmery, stiltwalking finery while Random, wearing a green outfit with a giant orange flower encircling his head approaches a baby in a stroller and begins doing froglike squat-jumps for the child's entertainment.

A group of Asian tourists, smiling, bustles over to have its picture taken with these hilarious creatures. Members of a wedding party, here to take advantage of the romantic beaux arts "ruins" that compose the Palace of Fine Arts, momentarily desert the bride and groom to also come have their pictures made with the Bantu freaks.

And the freaks couldn't be in finer form. Random, as the giant orange flower, seems incapable of holding still. He's jumping, twirling, balancing on one foot. He climbs up on a ledge of one of the ruins and, crouching, begins growling like a lion. A growling flower. Visitors strolling through the park point and laugh. Moondoggy, his balloon tendrils flapping crazily around his head, is on stilts too, and is urging children to run under his towering legs. He shouts, "*Kid power!*" and pumps his fists in the air every time a tentative two-year-old has the courage to dash through.

Paradox has abandoned the flowers in his ears, exchanging them for a long black leather trench coat and hat. His white painted face still has a circular pattern of fresh petals, though, causing him to look like a rather sinister incarnation of Vishnu. He carries a long ring-master's whip. "I see this man as a shaman," pronounces Moondoggy/Balloonhead. "and we are all the beings he has evoked—the spirit guides. He—"indicating Random the Growling Flower—"is from the plant world. I'm from the trippy ayuhuasca world and you two," he points to Natalia and Dalamah, "are the tribal aboriginal spirits."

More than one mythology is being evoked here. The most prominent, if unspoken one, is that of San Francisco's own 1967 summer of love—the myth that says if we paint our faces, wear crazy clothes, run wild in the streets and love everyone, world peace is sure to follow. The Bantu clearly are the next generation of artists/lovers/performers to inherit the mantle of that local wisdom. It's a beautiful myth made for playing out on a perfect sunny afternoon like this one.

"We're mainly doing this to raise consciousness," says Philippe, a multi-talented individual whose professional skills include chocolate truffle-making and web design. "We try to get not only the 'choir' but normal people in society to come and be transformed. We've been compared to Cirque du Soleil, not on skill level, but in terms of colorfulness and emotional effect. Usually we start with a story and then incorporate circus acts. These stories are always about raising consciousness, being eco-conscious and loving one another, how we as a community can grow and connect with communities around us. It's sort of like *Moulin Rouge*, with the whole bohemian-style values of Truth, Love and Beauty."

Add Fate to this triune, bohemian pantheon: belief in an invisible string that binds us all in a single destiny. No such thing as accidents. This is the "mystic" in Bantu Mystic Family. More than once, I overhear a Bantu performer deftly insert the phrase "as if there were such a thing" anytime the words "random" or "accident" come up. It's a nonchalant mantra, one that flows easily between people and is even used as a self-correcting device: "I was walking down the street and just randomly—as if there were such a thing—ran into this guy." This is so pronounced that when I am introduced to the person actually *named* Random (the Growling Flower), I immediately say, "As if there were such a thing." But the witticism falls flat: Random gives me a confused look.

My first brush with the group took place nearly two years prior, during a performance at San Francisco's Maritime Hall, a large two-story union hall for area dock workers. The air that night was chilled with the tinge of a coming autumn as an impatient crowd—we had been waiting for more than an hour outside—finally pressed through the double glass doors.

Past the entrance was a stairwell leading to the upper-floor performance space. A juggler stood on the landing, tossing colorful balls, while a didgeridoo player and Tibetan throat singer sent ancient vibrations echoing loudly through the improvised sound chamber. Upstairs, on the main stage, a young man was already weaving the crowd together into a unified yoga/tai chi dance. The sight of partygoers in full costume, suddenly forgetful of their attire, attempting to do graceful squats and turns, was priceless.

It soon became impossible to tell who was a performer and who was an audience member, as more and more people pressed into the room and DJs switched the room's tempo to an upbeat trance. Certainly the girl hanging upside down from her knees on a static trapeze while playing the violin was part of the scheduled entertainment. But the wandering clowns? The man with the giant hat? Poi-spinners twirled arcs of fire in the middle of the dance floor, seemingly oblivious to the hazard posed to the numerous costumes crowded in around them. Another, more impressive fire performer did a spectacular back flip off the stage while continuing to spin balls of flame. Downstairs, in the basement, an evil clown band played on a washtub bass and junkyard instruments.[1]

It was not until midnight that the full Bantu Mystic Family Circus made a thunderous entry to the accompaniment of large, handheld tribal drums. Monkey men, their torsos painted with brilliant markings of white, red and black, faces obscured by strange masks, gamboled around the drummers. A flock of white-garbed dancers, leather-wearing butoh dancer crocodiles, grandmother owls draped in feathers and shawls, and other exotic creatures followed. Multiethnic faces of black, brown and white blended with the multi-specied aspect of the crowd. The room erupted into a single joyous jumping.

And almost as suddenly, the drums died away. In the ensuing hush, one could actually hear the shifting of polyester costume fabrics and clicking of beads as hundreds of San Francisco hipsters sat down in a giant circle. The audience and performers joined in a series of *ohm*s in different tonal ranges, creating a ceremonial stillness and focus. Yin and yang, the four directions, the five elements and the eight natural forces were invoked, and homage paid to the radiant multiplexity of the Ten Thousand Things.

Tekeba Bantu, the African-American/Native American storyteller and co-founder of the circus, paced around the circle in a robe and turban, carrying a large rattle. "Now my children, may I have your attention please," he began, with poetic phrasing. "This is an ancient story, told thousands of years ago./I am an ancient teacher, and a jojo/And I want you to walk through this window/Through time, to meet a young man: Yambo Yate."

"Yambo Yate!" The crowd, engaged, repeated the name [*yam-bo ya-tay*] loudly among themselves, as if relishing the sound of a great joke or a great mystery.

The two-hour performance that followed traced the young hero as he passed several tests to obtain a Sacred Seed of Life with which to save his village. The entire enactment took place within the circle formed by the seated audience, rather than on the amply proportioned stage. Yambo, wearing a white loincloth and tribal markings defining his torso, spine and arms, met the choir of grandmother owls, whose strange, complex harmonies exhorted him to seek pearls of wisdom on his quest for the seed. The butoh crocodiles, in blacks and greens, slithered in a trance-like state. Hyenas, whooping and laughing, taunted the young hero. Shifting, chattering monkey men surrounded Yambo and engaged him in a capoeira battle, all the while keeping up a percussive, Balinese monkey chant.

After many such encounters, Yambo finally reached the Sacred Tree of Life, a gorgeously costumed young woman with branches jetting from her shoulders and fingers. Parched, on the verge of death himself, Yambo supplied his last drops of water to the Tree, who in turn offered him her life-giving root. Speaking in a trebly, distorted tree-voice, she then instructed Yambo

in the art of growing from a seed to reach
the stars. In celebration, fire-bearing temple
dancers, representatives of Yambo's Seven
Sisters, appeared and lit up the center circle
with their exotic, golden tribal jewelry,
burning trays of fire, and flashing eyes.

The ceremony was complete. It was 2 A.M.
and I felt both exhausted and uplifted, even
as someone switched the sound system back
into techno overdrive and the entire ensemble
seamlessly merged back into a dance party.
"As a participant in this ritual, you have been
granted a seed—of peace, of love, of awareness. Take this seed and spread it to the hearts
of all who need it . . . " read the program that
I stuffed into my coat pocket.

Not many such large-scale performances
have been completed since 2001 due to the
monumental size of the Bantu Family. But
even in subsequent smaller performances,
many of the themes seen in "Yambo Yate"
are present: an agonizing concern with the
current direction of humanity and a convic-
tion that bringing a variety of myths and
cultural traditions together in performance
will serve as an inspirational template for
bringing humans themselves together.

Bantu Mystic Family Circus was born in
1999 at an outdoor music festival along the
Eel River in Northern California.
Moondoggy introduced two of his friends to
each other late one night. One was
Carmenchu Caballero, a longhaired young
woman from the Philippines with a background in commercial producing and
directing. The other was Tekeba Bantu, then
in his late forties, a former Army colonel
turned itinerate Rainbow Family member.
Tekeba eloquently described his vision of a

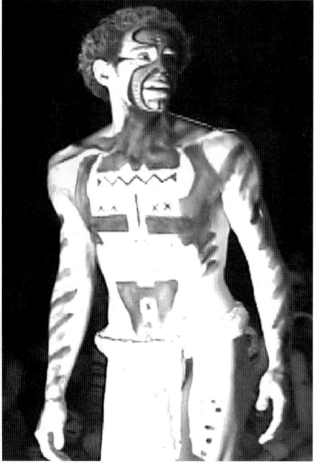

nomadic, healing arts circus during that initial meeting.

"Tekeba speaks in a language you can't quite explain," says Carmenchu. "That night he was speaking in terms of prophecies that for some reason rang true with me. And he did talk about a nomadic healing circus—not in those words but with those ideas—and I kind of looked around and said 'I'm surrounded by those people. *These* are the people you're talking about.'"

"A lot of people from the circus are artists that I've grown up with, we've all been hanging together for a while," she continues. "People were doing different things even before the Mystical Family Circus started. There was a desire to come together and recognize that San Francisco really is a big circus cauldron. We were already making music, making people happy. So we set up an organizational meeting of maybe seven or eight of us. It was easy in some ways to come together like that. It felt really blessed."

Tekeba's last name, Bantu, is the name of both a major language group in Africa (which includes Zulu and Swahili) as well as a philosophy of world brotherhood popularized by an early twentieth century human rights advocate. The name is composed of two syllables—*ntu*, which means "man" and *ba*, which means "all"—so that the word literally refers to all humankind. Bantu became the name of the group, not in deference to Tekeba, but to the philosophy of unification of mankind, with the initials coming to stand for Better Alliance of Nations Through Unity.

Tekeba also contributed the group's founding myth, "The Unity Story". The story is of an African king who took two people from each tribe and placed them on a piece of land to learn to work together and become a single, new tribe. Whenever there was war, these people would go out and stand arm to arm, link to link, to stop the war.

Tekeba formally recites the myth while sitting on a small sofa in Philippe's apartment, a few days after the group outing in the park. Now fifty-one, his large frame is animated in conversation, leaning forward to punctuate a remark or plopping backwards in stately languor against the sofa cushions, as now, during the recitation. A crocheted green and red Rasta cap tops his head, and thick, dreadlocked ropes hang down his back.

"Truth and Justice are sometimes blind," he says, "and when they are, they shed a tear."

> *All people came from the original seven tribes. When humanity cracked away from Woman, we cracked away from the Nyabingi (the heartbeat), and from all that we knew (nature).*
>
> *We understand that through Isis, the Golden Harp of Life, our dreams and visions are eternal. We also recognize that within our lineage is the Bird of Peace . . . {We} recognize that knowing the spirit of our ancestors is an ancient and powerful way of life. In this life we must band together for the betterment of humanity and work for a Better Alliance of Nations Through Unity . . .*

The recitation goes on, to include the coming of a future "Jesterworld" that will be populated by such wise fools as understand the mystic thread. "That's my story," Tekeba finishes powerfully. "And that is our mandate. To stand there."

To stand there. It was a mandate that the Los Angeles Police Department declined to recognize.

Tekeba's story instantly sparks recollections among the assembled Bantu members about their first, disastrous, performance of "Yambo Yate." It took place in March 2001, when the entire cast—acrobats, fire performers, musicians, puppets, birds, anansi spiders, butoh crocodiles, grandmother owls, temple dancers, *et al.*—made the pilgrimage to a warehouse in Los Angeles for what was to be the first public performance of the piece.

It was a party locale notorious for visitations from the fire marshal. Someone had listed "documentary film" as the purpose for obtaining the building usage permit—not a smart idea as it turned out. The troupe spent all day constructing two wooden stages in the space, erecting props, and preparing trays of vegetarian springs rolls and sushi for the evening's "love feast." As before, bands played and the gathering crowd engaged in a collective tai chi/yoga session. Suddenly the music stopped. The L.A.P.D. arrived and ordered everyone out.

Seven hundred people, including about 250 Bantu performers, balked at the police directive, taking refuge in sudden chaos. It wasn't hard, as nobody in particular was in charge.

"It was the kind of thing where they were looking for the leader. They were looking for the leader and there *was* no leader," recalls Paradox, who played the title character of Yambo Yate.

"So it was a big runaround for them; as soon as they thought they had found someone, suddenly that person would start acting like a total fool. They were looking to shut it down but it kept popping up in different sections."

At one point, a policeman got a working microphone and put it in someone's hands, commanding them to make an announcement to vacate the premises. The performer took the microphone—and a deep breath—and let go with a long, resounding *ohm*. Hundreds of people joined in, creating one huge cosmic vibration.

Eventually everyone was forced out, allegedly so the fire marshal could get a head count. What greeted them, according to Bantu member Deborah Tealma, was "at least six cop cars, more than a dozen officers, and a helicopter, cordoning off the entrances and barricading the whole block."

"Lit up by the police helicopter," she recalls, "and the glaring lights of the cop cars, the musicians continued to play, the clowns wailed big clown tears ('WAH WAH WAH') and the group chanted. A green marionette tried negotiating and the grandmother owls serenaded the L.A.P.D., informing them that 'great pearls of wisdom lie inside you' in three-part harmony. But instead of recognizing those pearls they insisted on just following orders, ordering dispersion of an illegal assembly."

The ritual ceremony became a raging street party instead, with clowns pitting their wiles against police in riot gear. The drum circle moved outside the barricades and hundreds of kids followed, dispersing and reconvening numerous times until the entire cycle seemed pointless.

"There was just this level of 'how long could we keep the circle open? How long could we keep the possibility of the rules changing?'" remembers Paradox. "There was definitely a feeling of 'okay, this is our first major event and we are taking on *the system*.'"

"Even," he admits, "if it was partially because we screwed up with the building permit."

Around 4 A.M., after the sound system, lights and altars had mostly been torn down, a surreal stream of circus people and devotees floated back through the door, recalls Deborah. The performance took place "in a scaled-down form, partially in the dark, absent the fire except for that which comes from within . . . We did the ritual simply because it needed to be done. For ourselves. For each other."

As dawn arrived, a solitary cast member stood outside with the unused tickets to the show, handing them out to the departing revelers as "admission to the sunrise."

Remembering it now, in Philippe's apartment, with glasses full of homemade absinthe, the troupe members are euphoric in their symbolic victory. But the short-term interaction with local law enforcement perhaps matters less than certain verities about the troupe that the incident highlighted.

One is confirmation of the circus performance (or a theatrical performance involving traditional circus skills) as an actual, bona fide ritual.

"We actually experience it as we present it," says Philippe. "That's why we're still around. It's not just about us getting together and freaking out. We realize we need this."

His words recall those of pioneering performance artist Mary Beth Edelson, who said in 1982, "An essential aspect of ritual [is that] we are experiencing and not just acting."[2]

Philippe, Paradox and some other members of the troupe actually met while participating in one of the renowned ritual performances of the Burning Man Opera (produced at the Burning Man festival by San Francisco artist/videographer Pepe Ozan). Characteristics of these performances include the setting of intentions through ritual initiations, and drawing on a widespread cast of "non-performers," which enables the performance to be less of a professional production than a community-based impulse. As part of the initiation to their own warrior cult, Philippe and Paradox both had to place metal-tipped arrows against their throats and break them using only the pressure of their bodies. Philippe still keeps a few unbroken arrows around as souvenirs.

Although Bantu performers range from amateur to highly skilled, they maintain a similar aspect of ritual by inviting interaction. "Anyone can walk in and be chorus," says Paradox. "We find space, opportunities, to create chorus from the entire audience." The audience, like the performers themselves, is invited to experience rather than simply observe.

One more parallel to ritual: Bantu members occasionally "draw" ritual circles, both in small gatherings and in the larger ceremonial context. If a circle can be opened to let more people/influences/cultures in, or ritually closed to set intentions, provide a

temporally defined set of relationships, invoke protection, is it so very odd that the form this theater would take is circus, the literal Latin meaning of which is circle?

Flexibility, or leadership-at-will, is another principle that was brought to the fore in L.A.

Instead of having leaders, per se, the Family operates on a principle of open collaboration. "In our giant collaborations we really make an attempt to do everything collectively, even scriptwriting," says Carmenchu. "I don't think any other theater piece has been created the way we've done it. In a single production there will be a lot of different choreographers, even different directors for different parts of the show."

A side benefit being that without leaders, the police won't know which responsible person to haul off to jail.

"In so many ways I feel like what we're about is that sense of crack training, being able to create things that respond intuitively," says Paradox. "It's getting an ensemble to be really intuitive and trust each other enough to know that, for example, Wyrd [another cast member] is leader for right now, Wyrd spoke up. Even if Wyrd doesn't get everyone to go 'Yes! we're doing that,' he'll get ten people to move in that direction. Sometimes that divides the group and makes madness happen. Sometimes those ten people are totally autonomous and get to do their own thing. That's what we've cultivated: the ability to create an immediacy.

"The question for me is, once we have that, how do we refine it into something that is able to reach a larger group of people?

So that it's not just for that group of people's fun or not just an action. How do we create theater performance that has resonance with the things that are going on in the world, as if we were an antidote for the poisons?"

Mystic Family Circus has as many meanings as it does members. On a more practical level, it has increasingly functioned as a talent network to match San Francisco's diverse talent pool with event producers. Cirque du Soleil in this way has hired a dozen of the Family for the last few years to add atmosphere to opening parties for its touring productions. The Montreal-based circus empire also hired some of the temple dancers to perform in its erotic circus production, Zumanity, in Las Vegas.

Simone Thayer is a blonde-haired goddess from the fire-dancing Apsara troupe, which borrows its name from that of the traditional Cambodian temple dancers. "Apsaras are channels to the gods," she says. "We just love the whole temple, compassionate wisdom through dance and sexuality thing. I'm both sacred and profane so it gives me a chance to be both."

"I admire Mystic Family Circus for being so open and letting people explore," she continues. "They are so huge and all-encompassing. Personally, I like it more condensed and concentrated." Which is one reason why Apsara, among other groups, continues to maintain an identity separate from MFC. "It makes for a sweeter brew. If you have all these different flavors coming in, who knows what's going to happen?"

"A lot of people have fine-tuned into smaller groups that do independent things," agrees Carmenchu. "People are always mixing it up; there's always a new crew coming together, there's fresh pieces being made all the time." Sometimes the group has a strong identity, as when mounting a major show like "Yambo Yate," while other times talents are dispersed in numerous directions. A few performers even question whether MFC qualifies for the name of "circus."

But Tekeba defends: "We are one of the premier circuses for peace and freedom. Our whole foundation is based on that. If, through our performances and our art and our music, we are constantly telling the truth with courage and compassion, then we're bringing a force out there that the people need right now. Ours is revolutionary as well as straight-up performance."

For co-founder Carmenchu, the Mystic Family Circus is a vehicle for eco-consciousness and community. She wants to promote a Filipino inventor who has developed technology that turns seawater into auto fuel. "We want to use circus as way to seek help and broadcast or at least investigate this," she says. "Eventually we want to travel in a bus that runs on seawater."

Her ecological community in the Philippines, called Dreamperch, is already coming to fruition. "It's my own personal land that I'm sharing with people," says Carmenchu. "The idea is that friends can come and build their own place."

"Once you're alone on an island you realize you want all your friends there," she observes. "The circus people are what inspired me. The people here come and mix with the tribes there—that's happening slowly, slowly. People who come help out, whether paying for food or picking up a saw and hammer." Carmenchu spends about four to six months each year building on her island. So far the eco-community features several small structures plus a central pavilion with a large kitchen for community dining.

Her comments highlight the fact that the new, underground circus can be as much about agenda as the traditional circus was about entertainment. It remains to be seen whether Mystic Family will fulfill its epic ambition to "travel to sacred and troubled lands" beyond Los Angeles, or if it will simply function as a family-like support network for a diverse group of entertainers.

"It's really about generating a culture, whether it be an information culture like Bindlestiff,[3] or whether it's an economical or ecological alternative like Mystic Family," adds Paradox.

"With Mystic Family the evolution feels like it's about meditation and the mystical ways. Who are the elders still teaching the mystical ways? How do we link up to learn the different systems like magical systems of alchemy, magical systems of cabbala, and magical systems of astrology? All of those things we can play with and embody because there's value in them. They wouldn't be as old as they are if there wasn't value in them. It's like vaudeville, the way Bindlestiff goes 'there's value in 1940s America.' And I think every circus family has its kung fu style or a form. What I want Mystic Family to be about is learning the forms that teach how to live in harmony, how to live in unity, how to live in song, and how to tap into creation collectively."

He sighs. "Yeah, it's really powerful work. I also feel like it's *old*. It's like the prehistory thing of *how did we hunt the mastodon*? How did we actually accomplish all of these impossible things? We did it by group mind, by telepathy. We did it by synching in with music and movement."

I am stomping up a darkened hill in San Francisco's Chinatown later that night, savoring the remnants of the evening: a bottle of homemade absinthe in one hand and an arrow in the other, and something like a wild portent of happiness for all mankind swirling around in my chest. Indeed, I have met the Bantu Family. May they live forever in light and love.

———————————⇒ɔ●ɕ⇐———————————

1. The Yard Dogs Road Show, Chapter 7

2. Levy, "Technicians of Ecstasy." p. 254.

3. Bindlestiff Family Cirkus, Chapter 8

7

YARD

DOGS

ROAD

SHOW

THERE'S AN ABANDONED old house off Highway 5, its sides half-gutted and wooden beams surrendered to the inevitability of decay. A beautiful broken-down house, the kind that sears your heart with a yearning wondering about the fate of old things, or simply a curiosity about whatever happened to the people who lived there, even as it becomes a speck in the rearview mirror of your car.

The Yard Dogs call this place the Source.

A black-and-white home movie captures the first visit of Eddy Joe Cotton, Five Liverd Larry and Voodoo Freddy to the Source. Five Liverd Larry, who in reality has but one liver and nine fingers, twangs on a Jew's harp on the front porch. Voodoo Freddy, in an undershirt and old jeans, makes percussive noise on a washboard nearby while Eddy Joe, the gentleman tramp, wears a white suit as he plays on a washtub bass. All three are wearing hats.

Says Miguel Strong (a.k.a. Freddy), "We said we'd start a jug band if we could find the right old house to use the front porch of. And there it was, looking like it had fallen from the sky."

The group pulled over in Eddy Joe's old Ford Galaxy 500 and Flecher Fleudejon (a.k.a. Larry) set up a video camera on a suitcase in front of the house.

"We played on the porch and then we went up and played in the attic. We played in that house for about four or five hours," says Eddy Joe. "Up in the attic there's a window and you can see these beautiful fields for ever and ever. Voodoo Freddy started nailing cans to his washboard, finding anything around the house he could play. That was our first rehearsal. That was the birth of it."

On that day Eddy Joe christened the group The Yard Dogs, and it was not long before the jug band expanded to include a burlesque show, a Mystic Man, a sideshow museum and much more. The entire group became the Yard Dogs Road Show, a road-happy love letter to another era writ in large, ecstatic letters on the trash blown off the highway by progress.

In fact, the group's name hearkens back to a time when progress was symbolized not by highways but by railroads. A yard dog is a hobo or train term for a particularly hard-working kind of locomotive that stays in the rail yards hooking trains together. The name is altogether fitting, because Eddy Joe himself is a hobo. A train-rider.

Eddy Joe hopped his first train at age nineteen in Denver, beginning a decade of free rides on the nation's railroads and introducing him to a vagabond subculture that most people assume disappeared along with the Great Depression. His early years on the rails are chronicled in a brilliant 2002 autobiography called *Hobo* and subtitled *A Young Man's Thoughts on Trains and Tramping in America*.

Now age thirty, Eddy Joe has a slight build, a shock of black hair and a face defined by high cheekbones surprisingly unscathed by his numerous days and nights spent out-of-doors and often out of work. Indeed, his good looks often evoke comparisons to a young Johnny Depp. For years after the Yard Dogs formed, Eddy Joe continued to ride freight, with the Road Show forming a kind of sidetrack to his main adventure.

"They hated me for that, they were like 'You started this damn thing, how come you're not into it all the time?' Well, because I'm a tramp," Eddy Joe laughs. "That's what I am *first*.

"One of my favorite things to do is hop off a train and walk down the main street of some small town at sunrise with just a couple blankets and a bottle of water. It's such a beautiful time because it's like the airwaves are free, the mass subconsciousness is clear wherever you are because everyone is snoozing—they're all in dreamland somewhere. And also there's no cars. When I found that and saw how beautiful life can be in that world, I knew that's where my heart was. I found something that was precious.

"My heart is also in the Yard Dogs," Eddy Joe continues. "Everyone in the Yard Dogs has that tramp/hobo spirit; that's what drew everyone together, that whole idea of travel and showmanship. I haven't ridden trains in two years but I'm on the road with the show a lot now, probably half the year. It used to be all the time, but it doesn't matter—I'm definitely still a tramp. All the old guys I met on trains always called themselves tramps."

The stage tonight at the Odeon nightclub in San Francisco looks as if a bunch of tramps had decided to pool their collective findings from a local junkyard. Several vintage suitcases hold spoons, a gong, a stepladder, antique cake tins, pot lids, a rack of bottles and a horn attached to a bicycle pump. A circular saw blade is painted with the group's motto, "Ride Free." The tiny stage is crowded with a washtub, brass instruments, plastic toys, and an old jack-in-the-box. I wonder aloud, what is it going to sound like when it all starts up?

"Like half a tumbleweed on a rusty roller skate," replies Mz. Lily Rose Love, the Yard Dogs' trombone player.

Lily, with her hazel eyes and fabulously long, thick, curly brown hair, is wearing a bowler hat, a polka dot dress and white spats tied over her black boots. The others continue to show up one by one. There's a skinny blond man with a whiskey jug and a grin. A swarthy, shirtless man wearing a parka and a bedraggled feather in his cap. A thin man wearing a white undershirt and a hat pushed back from his forehead, evoking the look of a 1940s union laborer. From under the brim of his own hat, Eddy Joe's face, boyishly charming in the sunlight, turns sharper, harder under the club lights. He looks like a card shark.

More junk arrives: a giant saloon painting of a naked lady reclining on a couch, a tire, a live chicken. The chicken, Pepper, pokes about on the main stage oblivious to the noise of the setup.

"We took it on tour with us this year," says Eddy Joe. "The chicken travels good. Sometimes it freaks out 'cause there's too many people around but mostly it's okay. We think it might be deaf."

There's another chicken running around the premises too, club owner Chicken John, founder of the self-styled punk rock Circus Redickuless. The impresario of what was once hailed by the press as the "Stupidest Show on Earth" has retired from touring to run The Odeon, a dive on Mission Street that often hosts circus-type performances. Right now Chicken is standing in front of the red and blue exterior of the Odeon, his round face and black-rimmed glasses sticking out of a brown western suit, impatiently waiting for a delivery of ice that got sent to the wrong club.

"I'm a facilitator of the arts now," says Chicken. "I'm not broke anymore, not so much of a con artist." Although, he assures, "I can still lie."

Chicken has held open auditions for the Jim Rose Circus at his club, and has even passed along a few tips to the master showman himself.

"I gave him the best act ever: flaming vomit. This guy would drink 151 proof alcohol straight, drink syrup of epecac and vomit onto a torch. When he was finished he would be backstage dry heaving. It was horrible, but the greatest thirty seconds of circus I've ever seen. Anyhow, Jim wouldn't take it 'cause it was too good."

Inside, Leighton Kelly (a.k.a. Hellvis) is carefully putting finishing touches to his cabinet of curiosities. The Norton P. Electric Sideshow Museum is draped in red fabric and tiny white lights, highlighting such rarities as a pair of two-headed lizards, a shrunken head painted to look like a clown, a mummified fairy and a set of teeth. The voodoo curse is labeled "Do Not Touch" and another, indefinable object is simply labeled "What is IT?"

Leighton, a charismatic artist with reddish blond curls, mutton-chop whiskers and a yellow silk flower in his lapel, is obliged to explain. "A friend of mine's a mortician," he says. "A lot of people are born with tails, but most get them cut off. This 52-year-old guy came in and he still had his tail, so my friend got it for me. Let's see . . . I got this eye at an auction for three bucks. It is one of the two original glass eyes belonging to Norton P. Electric himself. This calcified Devil Baby was found in an abandoned mine shaft of old Las Vegas . . . "

By the time he reaches the Claw of the Lizard King ("remnant of an ancient subcutaneous [sic] culture"), it's time for the show to begin.

The band starts and, not surprisingly, the syncopated clatter sounds as if an entire junkyard has decided to get up and go for a walk. Eddy Joe sings a song that proclaims him "King of the Hobos". The Black & Blue Burlesque girls do naughty things in shadow from behind a screen. The band picks up steam with the addition of electric guitar and Lily's trombone. On the main stage, Eddy builds a campfire and sits around with his "hobo" pals, who throw off their rags to reveal corsets, striped stockings and high heels. The Black & Blue Burlesque is wickedly sexy.

Tobias the Mystic Man is a jack-of-all-circus-trades whose anatomical specialties include the Human Blockhead and a trick called the Human Fountain (in which he drinks a large quantity of water and spits it out again in a continues stream). Tonight he swallows several swords and sabers for the audience's entertainment. Hellvis strips down to black leather pants and draws flaming torches across his bare chest before putting them out in his mouth. Guitarboy (Miguel/Voodoo Freddy) comes out wearing a suit of electric lights and makes some noise on a double-necked guitar. The crowd screams. Lily, whose birthday is at midnight tonight, belts out the blues ("If you don't want my peaches, then WHY do you shake my tree?").

It's an inspired combination of vaudeville, sideshow and noonday hilarity in a broken-down jalopy of a band, with the shadow of a light-footed tramp stepping through it all. The tramp and the clown collapse into each other onstage, reminding me of something Eddy Joe wrote earlier in his prologue to *Hobo*:

> *When a tramp is calling into the jungle {a hobo encampment}, it is very similar to a clown walking onstage. The tramp must have his spiel or his skit prepared . . . A clown will ride freight and a tramp will work under canvas. At times the clown and the tramp are one and the same . . . A showman will do whatever it takes to get his show to the next town. A tramp will do the same.* [1]

The show at the Odeon is the last of the Yard Dogs' summer tour and the crowd gathered about the stage is loud, enthusiastic and packed tight. Cowboy hats and corsets, tributes to the group's frontier fashion sense, are everywhere. Chicken John is forcing his way from the front of the club to the back door, where some over-eager fans, unable to get tickets, are trying to break in. Fights break out at both entries. The minute the Yard Dogs finish their last song, a pissed-off Chicken flips on the house lights and yells, "Everyone leave! Go home!"

* * *

The next day, Side Car Tommy is sitting at a kitchen table, receiving a tattoo from his bandmate Micha. The tattoo is a little round dot on the inner curve of his hand between the thumb and index finger.

"We do this at the end of every tour, it's like a punctuation," Tommy says. I look around and see that it's true; just about everyone has a sprinkling of dots across their wrists and fingers.

But this is Tommy's first one. Micha first swabs at the area with tea tree oil—"I try to go as natural as possible," he says—and then quickly begins jabbing with a sewing needle dipped

in black India ink. It's a jailhouse tattoo, the type that quickly fades to green.

Tommy, the Yard Dogs' drummer, is a study in relaxation although the procedure obviously hurts. Micha, barefoot and shirtless, is bent over his hands, his waxed moustache stiffly standing away from his cheeks. The group's guitarist has sideburns, a wide Mohawk and skinny black pigtails that hang down behind his ears tied with scraggly feathers. He looks like a white fur trapper who has spent too much time fraternizing with the Indians. On the table next to them are three bottles of Jim Beam, two of them empty and one well on its way to being so. Plus a potted plant, a toy Eldorado and a bottle of vitamin C. A black and yellow dog criss-crosses the kitchen floor.

Lily is telling me about her first encounter with the Yard Dogs.

"When I was fourteen I went to San Francisco for the first time and I was staying in the second floor of a flat overlooking the courtyard of this big biker warehouse crazy art scene. It was the most lively thing going on. So I was spying and hanging out and talking to really interesting people and there was this one beautiful blond boy that I kind of had a crush on.

"One night I was braiding my hair at the window and he came roaring up on a motorcycle, looked up at me and said 'Rapunzel!' and climbed the drainpipe, kissed my hand, did a backflip down, jumped on his motorcycle and roared off. And then I never saw him again, until seven years later. I was walking on lower Haight Street and a couple of people painting a building looked vaguely familiar as I walked by. And the dark-haired

YARD DOGS ROAD SHOW

one said, 'I think I met her at a Rainbow gathering, but that was five years ago.' And I was thinking, 'I was at that gathering,' but I was kind of embarrassed because I don't go to those anymore. I turned around and went back and it was Eddy Joe. And he said, 'My friend remembers your name, it's Lily, right?' And it was Miguel, the one who kissed my hand."

Miguel apparently hasn't lost any of his wild energy since that first meeting. He has a penchant for jumping out of or on to moving vehicles, sometimes chasing down city buses and hopping on the back fender, feet dragging. Once he chased down a street cleaner, climbed on top and received third-degree burns on his arms from the steam.

"It's his madness and his power," says Leighton, speaking of Miguel. "It's what fuels the show but it can also be kind of scary sometimes." Like the time Voodoo Freddy decided to spit fire using gasoline (most fire performers use kerosene or lamp oil) and generated a huge fireball that also burned his face.

"I have a crazy life, it's really wild," says Miguel. "One day I thought I really was going crazy and my mom said 'No, you're not crazy, you're an artist.' And I was like, 'Thanks.'"

Of course Miguel couldn't resist hopping trains for a while with Eddy Joe; neither could the other original member of the Yard Dogs, Flecher Fleudejon. But for Flecher, an art teacher, daredevil feats take more of a back seat to making films. The footage he captured on 8 mm at the Source was eventually incorporated into a larger documentary that tells of the mythological coming together of the Road Show. Another short film, "Holy Clown," shows a tramp (Eddy Joe) who is baptized in a river and reborn as a red-nosed clown. The entire troupe amuses itself by making movies with Flech in the spare time on tour.

Emily Hughes, founder of the Black & Blue Burlesque, initially came to the Yard Dogs as Miguel's girlfriend. "The Yard Dogs didn't really have a female element," she says. "So we created this little silly burlesque."

Emily, who works as an exotic dancer in real life, was the only female performer in the beginning except for Lily (who calls herself "one of the boys"). "Then the other girlfriends started to come on tour. If they weren't musicians they really didn't have much to do, so we tried to put them in and get them involved," she recalls. "So it kept growing and growing and at some point it became a really important identity for us, the women."

Now the group is polished enough that they are starting to perform outside of the Yard Dogs as well. "We've been doing a lot of burlesque research, and we take our inspiration from the 1880s," says Emily. "Burlesque started in the 1880s more as theater. It was a big deal because women would wear tights to play men's roles. The first burlesquers were women that were writing and performing their own shows, which was also really unheard of at the time. We stumbled on the whole Barbary Coast thing . . . it's absolutely fascinating."

Sometimes being a member of the Road Show "is very emotionally trying," she continues. "Like Miguel and I used to be together and now we're not. He tried to replace me with his new girlfriend! I had to fight tooth and nail to keep my foot in it and it was definitely a hard decision; I had to ask myself why I was subjecting myself to this, to be in it and be broken up with him. It's hard to stay friends with an ex-lover, much less work and perform with them. But we did it. It meant so much to me, the Yard Dogs. It's a lot of work but there's so much love in it we just wouldn't have it any other way. You go on tour and find yourself in the most amazing situations and have memories with your dearest friends."

Ah, memories. The group recalls a time on this tour when Miguel showed up at one of their gigs wearing only his underwear and a hat, saying, "What does a guy have to do to get a drink around here?" Says Lily, "We took pictures; actually we made him hold my chicken and stand on stage for a long time while we *pretended* to take pictures."

Eddy Joe remembers an encounter in Las Vegas with a character named Vanilla Fudge.

"We were doing a show in Las Vegas—we always stop in Vegas—at the only bar we could get in to downtown. A friend of ours was bartending there. We're setting up and here comes this 45-year-old black man dressed in a full three-piece peach suit. He introduces himself before the show and says 'Hi, I'm Vanilla Fudge and I would like to perform with you.' We said 'You're more than welcome to get up on stage and do whatever you do.'"

As the night progressed, the Yard Dogs noticed their new friend gradually getting more and more drunk—heavily drunk, in fact. "So about halfway through our show I'm on the microphone and I hear him behind the curtain going 'Psst—hey—give me the mike! C'mon, give the mike!'" Eddy Joe says. He introduced him, "Ladies and gentlemen—Vanilla Fudge!"

"So I hand him the mike and he comes bouncing out behind the velvet curtains in his full peachy suit. He starts doing this James Brown thing—'Hey-yo-hey'—all that stuff. After about seven or eight minutes of that I get the mike back and he sits down on the end of the stage, passes out and stays there for the remainder of the show. But every once in a while, at just the right moment, he'd wake up and go 'Hey—yeah—get on the goodfoot!'"

The Yard Dogs have performed in a number of interesting places, including, but not limited to, the parking lot behind the Denver County jail, Indian reservations, and smack in the middle of the blacktop surface of Route 66 in Arizona.

"That's the interesting thing, there's all these different groups that come out of the Bay area, most of them haven't managed to travel, to be a traveling show," says Eddy Joe. "They're just kind of doing big raves in San Francisco. But every time I have a conversation with anyone who's in these groups I always say 'Put it on the road.' 'Cause there's a lot of people out there who don't have what we have here.

"I'm not talking about getting on a bus and traveling across the country trying to change people's lives," he clarifies. "Who am I to say that? It's not my role in this world. But I know that by providing a great show and solid entertainment people are going to have a hell of a good time. That's where I agree with Charlie Chaplin. He had a social agenda but his art was brilliant and it transcended so many different boundaries. You wouldn't sit through one of his movies and think, 'This guy's dogmatic, he's trying to shove something down your throat.' You'd just be laughing your ass off."

"I love this country," he adds. "The hobo represents patriotism to me in a very grassroots way, without the dogma."

Eddy Joe Cotton is not his real name. He made it up on his first day out jumping trains as a kind of alias to travel by: "Cotton" from the sight of clouds in Wyoming, "Joey" the traditional name for a clown. From the beginning, the tramp carried a clown in his back pocket.

"There was a realization I came to when I was traveling," says Eddy Joe. "There were a lot of moments that were profound, they changed my whole life and the way I look at everything; it destroyed who I was and then I rebuilt this other identity. But I realized at one point that I'd found something that was very special. I guess it was freedom. And the next step was to try to share it."

———⟫⟩◉⟨⟪———

1. Eddy Joe Cotton, Hobo (New York: Three Rivers Press, 2002) p. xxiii.

8

FAMILY

BINDLESTIFF

CIRCVS

8

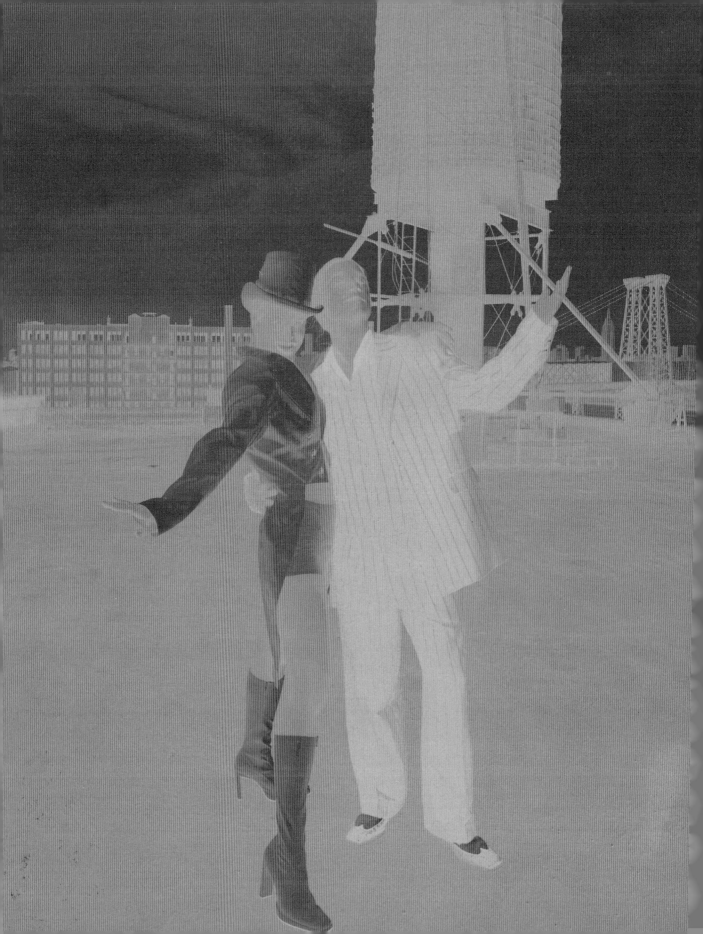

KINKO IS A drunken, masturbating, butt-sniffing, trashcan-digging, degenerate sort of clown. Not the sort you'd necessarily encounter at a Ringling Bros. show, although there's something about the guileless tramp character, with his painted-on five o'clock shadow, that brings to mind the beloved former Ringling clown Emmett Kelly. Kinko wears a rope noose around his neck as a fashionable accessory to his shabby suit and oversized shoes. He reels, drops into a chair and opens a porn magazine to its center spread before falling into an alcohol-induced slumber.

To his right, a pretty girl in a white fluffy prom dress appears. Another noose hangs from the ceiling. She approaches, lays her head backwards through the noose so that it rests at the base of her skull. As carnival music plays, lightly, almost childishly, the rope lifts and pulls her into the air. She spins slowly and then faster, a miracle of balance and poise, as the prom dress is drawn higher and higher by centrifugal force. Which is more astounding: the way a human neck can withstand such torque or the way her hemline is headed for the ceiling? For a few seconds the dress lifts completely, amusing the club patrons by revealing a complete lack of underwear. Then the white lace drops over her muscled thighs, the girl gracefully returns to earth and disappears backstage.

Kinko wakes up. We have been given a peep into the pornographic dreams of a clown.

It's hard to describe the ineffable charm of this particular skit, which comes across as more fanciful than sexual. It starts one thinking about the appeal of a girl in a white dress, spinning. What else would we expect a clown to be aroused by? Certainly not a conventional centerfold. It seems more likely that Kinko gets off by thinking about butterflies. Despite his moral character, there's a part of him, as a clown, that appeals to innocence. He is as whimsical as he is repugnant.

Ringmistress Philomena, however, is *not* a study in paradox. She strides across the stage on long legs wrapped in wickedly laced, high heeled boots, giving slow-moving clowns a smart nudge *au posterior* with a nicely pointed leather toe. Her getup is hot pants, a top hat and matching tails. She is every man's dream—or nightmare—a redhaired vixen who knows how to handle a whip and has enough attitude to divide and distribute amongst any other females present.

Philomena is Stephanie Monseu, one of the two founding members of the New York-based Bindlestiff Family Cirkus. The other founder is her romantic and artistic partner Keith Nelson, a.k.a. Kinko, a.k.a. Kinkette, a.k.a. Mr. Pennygaffe. Together they lead a merry band of whip crackers, knife throwers, stilt walkers, aerialists, contortionists and clowns. The exact lineup changes from show to show, but the parental duo of the perverted clown and his dominating mistress remains the same. Since its founding in 1994, the Bindlestiff Family Cirkus has served as a nexus for circus performers in New York, and a major force in the citywide revival of old-fashioned entertainments like vaudeville and burlesque.

The pair met while waiting tables at a 24-hour restaurant in downtown Manhattan. "We both worked the graveyard shift, serving hash browns at 5 A.M. to club kids who would come out all dazed in the sunlight after having danced all night," Stephanie recalls. "When it was slow we would go into the back alley and eat fire."

She smiles. "I begged and begged him until he finally taught me." And so he did. And so they fell in love.

The two formed an erotic fire performance act called Fireplay that they worked in the city's adult cabarets, S&M clubs and fetish balls. They experimented with body modification and live piercings, strung chains connecting their piercings and used them to suspend large bowls of fire. "We were testing boundaries and just seeing what the body could do," says Keith. "I had second and third degree burns from exploding handcuffs that happened a little too early in the act. Steph at that point had broken her arm and had all these pins and needles holding them together—we'd sometimes use them as a fire prop and shoot fireworks off them."

They took a week-long trip to New Orleans to perform on the street, where they began to get an inclination of where their new-found skills might take them. In 1994, New Orleans was destination central for transient performer-types. "These street punks would travel around from city to city living off of spare change," says Stephanie, "and a lot of them were eating fire and doing crazy stunts to get pocket change. So we met each other in New Orleans.

"There was a band there called The Daffodils and they were doing crazy mask-making and giant, costumed stilt-dancing, and parades with fire spinners and Balinese dancers. And it was that kind of do-it-yourself, jubilation-in-the-street ethic that really struck me and Keith and made us feel that we wanted to put something together."

But it wasn't until they visited Burning Man for the first time later that year that they committed to forming the circus. It was there, in the carnivalesque mosh created by performers, artists and lifestyle lovers of the absurd, that they encountered punk circus' leading man, Chicken John.

The founder of Cirkus Redickuless was sitting in the middle of the Black Rock desert, away from the festival, burning his circus tent.

"We were wandering through the desert late one night, lost, and we saw a campfire," recalls Stephanie. "And it was Chicken John burning his circus tent because he had just had such a disastrous tour. He was literally burning the tent. We walked up to this thick, billowing, acrid, fuming cloud of smoke and he's like 'Who the hell are you? Come on, join me!' And he passed around a jug of High C and vodka and that's where the first tour was born."

Stephanie picked the new troupe's name out of a thesaurus. "Bindlestiff" is a slang word for hobo, referring to the tramp's traditional bundle-on-a-stick form of luggage. Keith and Stephanie had fantasized from the beginning about taking a circus show on the road, so Bindlestiff seemed appropriate.

The first Bindlestiff troupe was composed primarily of performers the couple had met through the underground erotic scene of New York, with a few other additions. Baby Dee, a transvestite, was the bandleader and played accordion. David Didd, the person who taught Keith juggling in college in exchange for a bottle of whiskey, was also invited on tour, along with a trumpet player and a magician. Stephanie's sister Lorraine rounded out the group and started two special traditions: bug-eating and the Autonomadic Bookmobile.

The insectivore act is not a pretty one, but it is best when performed by a pretty girl. There's something about the spectacle of soft, feminine, kissable lips sucking down writhing earthworms or clasped firmly around the carapace of a beetle that can really be counted on to draw a reaction from the audience. But the Bindlestiffs equally enjoyed the reaction they got from distributing radical books and 'zines along with the show.

"In the beginning it was myself, Keith, a rubber chicken and a box of books," says Stephanie. "That was always part of the dream too, to have a vehicle to haul radical literature around and create an alternative lifestyle midway, getting people to get together and exchange ideas as activists."

Stephanie is sitting on a couch in her apartment as she recalls this, wearing black jeans and a black T-shirt with a pink "Velvet Hammer Burlesque" logo. Her dark red hair is loose and the T-shirt exposes the colorful tattoo work that wraps both her arms. Her couch, indeed her entire apartment, is located inside of a Williamsburg, Brooklyn warehouse, in a corner of the small radical press Autonomedia. Keith began working here after he graduated with a degree in anarchist studies from Hampshire College, trading living space in exchange for a salary. The headquarters of the Bindlestiffs is reached only after walking past rows of high shelving piled with titles such as *Marxism Beyond Marxism* and *Psychedelics ReImagined*.

The relationship between the Bindlestiffs and Autonomedia was always close. From a couple of books with props, though, Lorraine bumped the concept up during the first tour to an actual sideshow where books were hawked with the zeal of a carnival barker. The Autonomadic Bookmobile eventually got its own truck, painted in a riot of orange, yellow and blue, and two regular performers: Dr. Henceforth Flummox and Dr. Okra P. Dingle, who walk on glass and pound nails in their noses in-between book sales.

"In Cedar Rapids, Iowa, they were parked outside the venue we were playing at," says Stephanie. "Two local beat cops walked up to them, watched their show and pronounced them devil worshippers. And told them to leave. We're talking about two gypsy-costumed performers walking on nails. The issue of public space in America, especially in cities, is a highly charged issue. Vendors on street corners getting busted by cops because they don't have the right permits. The issue of being able to sell books—there are first amendment rights associated with that. There's the idea that entertaining on public space, even if you're not doing it for money, is a public nuisance or a public safety issue.

"It seems that especially in New York, when you have people assembling it causes fear. People are talking to each other, sharing ideas, it's a big unorganized entity and that's not encouraged. The Bookmobile has taken that to task."

The Bindlestiffs waited anxiously to join Circkus Redickuless for their first outing across the open fields of America. But Cirkus Redickuless, a twenty-person ensemble that in every way lived up to its name, didn't make it.

"I think one of their performers was in jail, one was in rehab, one had a broken hand—we had to do the first two weeks without them," says Keith. "By then our performers were used to getting paid after every gig. When we joined up with Chicken, getting paid ended for the next month and a half. We drove a thousand and some miles from North Carolina to finally meet up with Redickuless, and did a show for four punk rockers in Pflugerville, Texas.

"And so began the tour. There were twenty-five people and three vans, two of which broke down every single day. There were many nights that we made two hundred bucks to try to feed twenty-five people, which meant bologna sandwiches with no condiments many nights. It was amazing—in a short period of time we learned everything *not* to do on tour and I can't ask for a better education than that month and a half. I owe Chicken dearly for that lesson."

The Bindlestiffs were a full-on, often visceral, adult-oriented circus. One of their earliest finale pieces featured Keith and Stephanie in clown white makeup and clown bibs. They would sew big pom-poms directly on to each other's chests, drawing blood, then paint clown makeup on each other with blood, go into a little mime sequence and "die" onstage.

Stephanie became adept at precision whip cracking. She also developed a notorious plate-spinning routine, balancing on her shoulders and holding up a pole inserted in her vagina. She says she doesn't relate to the occasional complaint that the act is degrading to women. "I'm proud of that act," she says. "I'm probably the only woman in the world who does that act outside of Taiwan. Definitely the only woman to perform it in Cleveland, Ohio."

Her character, Ringmistress Philomena, then and now provides the glue that holds the various acts of the Bindlestiff Cirkus

together, in an ongoing narrative rife with sexual innuendos and patently silly double entendres. She vamps around, tossing her hair, teasing. "Sometimes I'll stop and look at everybody in the audience and make them wait," she says. "I like that tension. It's really just wanting to stay on top of the crowd."

Not that she doesn't already have everyone's rapt attention when she flicks a rose out of an audience member's teeth using her bullwhip, or when she's threading a condom up her nostril and out her mouth. Ringmistress Philomena is irreverent, raunchy, salty and, as Stephanie herself says, "not afraid to take a pie in the face. She definitely represents the most brazen and confident aspect of myself, who I'm not all the time. Really. I *wish* I could be her all the time."

As for Keith, "You can't have a circus without a clown," he says, "so Kinko definitely came on early in Bindlestiff history.

"In the beginning I was basically working on what I'd seen in video and just kind of working on my concepts of funny. I spent a good five to seven years finding the clown within, I guess you'd say. As time went on I was giving the props more and more a life of their own and creating a relationship with them. Like my whole relationship with the trashcan—everything comes out of it and goes back in. Kinko in a sense is living out of the trashcan. With Bindlestiff being the word for vagabond, I put myself in the perspective of the traveling hobo. He's definitely down on his luck, definitely the butt of every joke, but he finds a jovial nature to push through life."

Keith developed another character, Mr. Pennygaffe, a sort of urbane snake oil salesman-type, to highlight his sword-swallowing skills. Wearing his long black hair in a ponytail and a pinstriped suit, Mr. Pennygaffe reassures his audience before swallowing a lit neon tube: "Ladies and gentlemen, for those of you who know me, you know that I am adept at swallowing long objects. For those of you who don't know me—I'll see you in the bathroom after the show."

"I moved to sword-swallowing because fire-eating is not very good for you," says Keith. "Sword-swallowing, as long as you keep the swords clean, is better than fire-eating—as long as you don't fuck up. For me, sword-swallowing was something that would take dedication. Fire-eating you either get very early on or you don't. Blockheading you can get very easily. Sword-swallowing is like trapeze or juggling five balls: you either give up or decide to devote a major chunk of time to getting it." Keith practiced putting chopsticks down his throat every day for two years before he was able to control the gag reflex enough to move on to larger objects.

The Bindlestiffs departed the company of Chicken John and reconvened in New York where they met a significant new troupe member in the guise of a seven-foot-tall, 250-pound gay rabbit. Scotty the Blue Bunny, clad in a skintight Lycra bodysuit and seven-inch high heels, prepared to hop his way into the hearts of hundreds, even thousands.

"His thing was to walk into places all over America with us and just have people look at him," says Stephanie, waxing sentimental over the thought. "He used to say if you've never seen a faggot before, if you've never seen a man in heels before, here's your chance. I'm not afraid to meet you halfway; I'm not afraid to look you in the eyes and say 'I'm a big, blue bunny.' There were towns where that was very risky."

"I was performing mainly as a poet and a performance artist experimenting with a lot of drag when I met Stephanie," says Scott Grabell, a.k.a. Scotty the Blue Bunny. His voice, indeed his entire demeanor, is as irrepressibly buoyant as one might expect of someone with a bunny alter-identity. "She asked me if I wanted to do a circus. So I showed up one day and I saw all these people eating fire and walking on glass and doing all this fantastic stuff. And I thought, wow—I can put on false eyelashes but I want to *fly*!"

Scotty learned how to juggle, eat fire and walk on a ball. The bunny costume came about by accident. He left his house one day wearing rabbit ears, on a whim, and some unknown person on the street yelled out delightedly, "Bunny!"

"And that was it, I became the Bunny," Scotty says. "There was a gender transformation also, I stopped doing drag. I stopped affecting a female persona and got rid of the makeup and just started wearing bunny suits. I kept the high heels, though!"

Scotty is an outsized personality who delights both in singing songs and throwing hilarious insults to the audience. In conservative mid-Western towns he takes naked wine baths onstage, throws grapes at the crowd and bestows an "Honorary Homosexual" award each night, usually to the most clearly uncomfortable male audience member in attendance.

"I just decided that since we were in all these straight places I was gonna make someone gay," says Scotty. "I get up on stage and I ask 'How many people in the audience are straight? How many heterosexuals are here tonight?' There's a big roar, gigantic applause. And I'm like, 'How many people are gay?' Crickets. And I say 'Well, that's not enough.'"

Scotty asks his volunteer a few indecent questions and then presents his award. "I have a lovely little certificate, with my picture, and it says the bearer of this document has been certified to be an honorary homosexual in good standing. I make the audience call them a faggot, and just before I give them the award there's an initiation and I pull out a Gatorade bottle which I call Scotty the Blue Bunny's Blow Job Desensitization Program, because it feels like a cock but tastes like a sports drink. So I make them get on their knees and drink the Gatorade. I just get crazy."

Says Keith, "I think the amazing thing about circus for radical politics is that there's a safety zone for the audience. An audience member can have a tranny sitting on his lap, even if he's homophobic, and for just a moment accept this is reality because this is circus. We come into some small town and everybody is looking at us, just waiting for us to do something wrong so they can kick our ass. But the moment they hear that we're a circus it makes it okay."

Scotty himself has never been the subject of hatred or had to engage in self-defense while on tour, which he points out is a good thing. "How much more pathetic could I be? I'm thirty-seven years old, college-educated and overweight in a skin-tight Lycra bunny outfit in high heels. I couldn't get away from you if I tried!"

"What's interesting about Bindlestiff is that in the beginning it was half about learning to do all these strange circus acts, but it was also about a parade of stunning personalities," Scotty observes. "Stephanie was the tattooed domineering woman, Keith was the long-haired, laid-back, pierced-beyond-belief sweetheart, and we had the big homo and the tranny and the runaway kid and the punk rock girl. Kids in warehouses in Georgia met this bunch of sexually aggressive, hairy, smelly, so-called circus performers and it just blew their minds."

The runaway kid joined after seeing the Bindlestiffs perform at a Sluggo's, a punk club in Pensacola, Fla. Daniel Smith, a.k.a. Daniel the Rubber Boy, asked if he could be on stage for a minute. "It was his first time on stage but he has a naturally very bendable body and just blew us away in a minute or two," says Keith. "The next day we're in New Orleans and we get a call that this kid has given away all his belongings and is in town looking for us and demanding to be with the show. After a bit of discussion he jumped in the van. We were wondering about feeding an additional person at that point, though he doesn't eat much. We also wondered how healthy it was to bend like that. At that point he had never understood warming up, stretching or exercising, because he'd never been in the performing realm, he just had this natural ability."

Since then, Daniel has trained extensively, spending a good deal of time at the San Francisco Circus School and moving on to a full-time professional career as a "bender." "When we met him he was a floppy little eighteen-year-old, and now he's pretty ripped and has the strength to hold a handstand," says Keith proudly.

During the early shows, lots of audience members were welcomed onstage.

"People would just show up and get freaky, just freak out because there was all this stuff going on," says Scotty.

"One of the best things I ever saw was one time at the Brooklyn Brewery. This girl comes out and says she's a contortionist. She's got this crazy music and starts doing her weird yoga referential contortion on the cement floor and then all of a sudden she shoves her entire fist in her mouth! The crowd went wild and she was like 'I never did that before!' Here's this girl bent like a pretzel on a concrete floor who's inspired to put her whole hand in her mouth and what does she get? A standing ovation. You don't have to be Britney Spears. You can have these great personal moments of being appreciated just for being energetic and spontaneous."

The wild energy of the Bindlestiffs began acting as a magnet to a different breed of performer, world-class entertainers who saw a chance with the group to push their creative boundaries. Una Mimnagh, the aerialist who performs as the girl in the white dress with Kinko, is also a featured star of the more mainstream Circus Flora in St. Louis. Una can easily command $1,500 or $2,000 a week instead of the $200 offered by the Bindlestiffs. But she says touring with the Bindlestiffs offers the perk of more creative freedom.

"People come to work with Bindlestiff because they don't like being told what to do," she says.

Ironically, the next time I see Stephanie, she is in the midst of telling a performer what to do.

Ultimately someone has to be in charge, and Ringmistress Philomena, with her

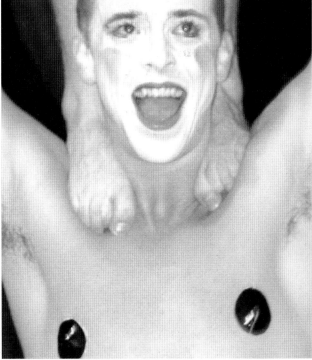

direct and unabashed demeanor, is eminently suited to the task. She has no qualms about telling the current aerialist (Tanya Gagne, of the neo-burlesque, acrobatic Wau Wau Sisters) to change her music as the group sets up for a production of "High Heels and Red Noses" in Austin, Texas. Meanwhile, two Ringling Bros.-trained clowns, Adam Kuchler and Matthew Morgan (the Slapinski Brothers) idly juggle pins and balls to warm up.

"There's as many different clowns as there are people," says Adam, a short, slight-figured man in his twenties. "Happy people, sad people, grumpy people, drunken hobos."

"The Russian clowns are serious, dramatic," says his taller partner, Matthew. "They're like the clowns in Cirque du Soleil's 'Allegria'. Did you see that? Their clowns are very poetic and dramatic. Their clowns think about death."

"My clown drowns in a pool of non-comedy," Keith wisecracks across the stage. Giggles all around at the thought of a hopelessly unfunny clown.

"It's good to have as many dimensions as possible," resumes Adam. "You don't want to be unaffected by things. You have to be open to everything around you—the audience, the band—and be able to react to that. Because if it's a real window to your soul, that's what people love. What does Keith say, a clown needs turmoil? A clown needs conflict? A clown needs conflict."

Later, Adam's clown routine brings down the house through the ingeniously simple device of putting his body through a 99-cent shopping bag, butt first. It's a piece that expresses a single, simple emotion:

glee. Tears roll down many a cheek as he hops about like a hermit crab onstage, butt and torso covered by a bag, gay little red-socked feet and waving hands still moving to the music.

Outside in the lobby, Miss Construe (Ellia Bisker) greets the evening's audience from behind a table spread with circus T-shirts, postcards and press-on tattoos.

"Traditionally the merch girl is the bugeater," says Miss Construe, a slender girl with soft brown hair and enormous glittery false eyelashes glued to her lids. This past winter she curried favor with the Bindlestiffs by showing up every weekend in costume at their variety show on New York's 42nd Street. When the Bindlestiffs got ready to go on tour, they invited their favorite groupie to come along as tour assistant. But as Ellia has discovered, with merchandising comes responsibility—of the multi-legged variety. Will she take up her designated role and munch a few bugs for the sake of Cirkus?

"I'm still weighing my options," Ellia smilingly says. Bat-bat go the giant eyelashes, as trembly as moth wings.

Getting ready for a three-month tour such as this one entails three to five weeks of furious, non-stop work, according to Stephanie.

"I'm on the phone, faxing contracts back and forth, rushing to the post office, making sure posters go out to seventy-two cities, sewing things, packing things, looking for shit you packed away last year and think you're going to use this year, finding out that it's broken and going across town to replace it," she says. "There's so much tension. When everything is finally packed in the trailer and the trailer doors shut, we're all looking around at each other going 'Ready? Ready?'" A Moorish orthodox priest who lives in their warehouse comes down and says a blessing, and the troupe pours a bottle of malt liquor over the van.

"That moment of turning the key in the ignition is just . . . " A sigh of pleasure from Stephanie replaces the descriptive. "I usually want to drive the first leg. I love leaving and I love coming back. Coming back to see the altered skyline after 9-11 was one of the most memorable events of my life."

It seems that the Bindlestiffs have more and more come to personify that famous skyline, at least in terms of its associations with old-fashioned entertainment. During the winters of 2002-04, notably, they ran the Palace of Variety and Free Museum at 125 West 42nd Street, in what was believed to be the first continuously running vaudeville show on Times Square in seventy years.

All their friends came. There was Jennifer Miller, bearded lady, social activist and founder of Circus Amok, juggling her machetes and ranting about national health care. There were the young talents from Coney Island's Sideshows By The Seashore, looking to keep their skills up during the off-season. Performers with the Big Apple Circus and Cirque du Soleil graced the stage. Over the course of two seasons, nearly 300 acts had a turn at the Palace of Variety, everything from kazoo players to the Mammy Project, a one-woman show examining the one hundred-year-old icon of Aunt Jemima.

The Free Museum contained more odes to the entertainment past of the district. There were programs from minstrel and vaudeville shows on Broadway, some of Harry Houdini's magic props, and a couple of objects from Hubert's Dime Museum, formerly located on 42nd Street, as well as about two dozen photographs that documented the architectural development of Times Square. The display also included ancient jars of deformed human fetuses, the likes of which old sideshows presented (for an extra dollar) as the blow-off. The fetuses' antiquity may have been uncertain, but they were authentic. (Many sideshows presented rubber copies instead, which were referred to as "bouncers.") During the last season, someone unsealed a jar and stole one of the babies. It was still 42nd Street after all.

"There's a big movement right now not just to circus but to sideshow and burlesque, and there's a lot of crossover between the groups," notes Keith. "Live entertainment in 2003 and onward is a phenomenal feat, to create an atmosphere that's based on human interaction and activity, the human body doing amazing things."

Though many performers in the New York scene are, in a postmodern sense, hearkening back to the golden age of live performance, the circus artists in some ways remain distinct, according to Scotty the Blue Bunny.

"The circus naturally gears you to a certain kind of performance," Scotty notes. "The circus is about opulence and indulging your audience in this visual ecstasy. Your visual skills have to be very strong to get across as a circus performer. You do find great athleticism in there. But half the battle is knowing how to enter and leave.

"The circus people really developed their own style whereas, there is a fashion to bur-lesque," he continues. "The burlesque girls are hung up on one image and one style of per-former. But you take a circus fire-eater: Keith and Stephanie worked the eroticism, Lila and Flambeau have great big art installations that they set on fire and it's a whole rock 'n roll energy. I sit and politely eat fire. There's these distinct styles. In the circus their personalities were so strong that even the stupidest prop from the 99-cent store could be transformed into an act. There was such a strong performative quality to things that you would find at a circus show. You transcend the body."

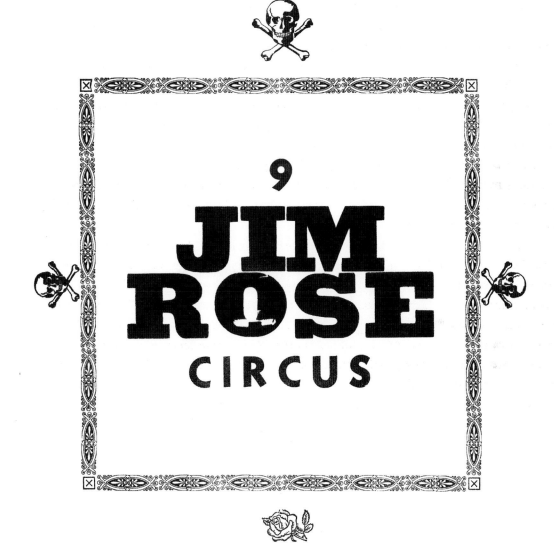

"HIS MOTHER WAS a Siamese twin that moved to England so the other one could drive...

"His father was a Philippine contortionist known as the Manilla Folder...

"He's got hair—in places—monkeys don't! While giving birth, his mother almost died from rug burn! Getting out of his mother was his first escape. Every time he got to the light in the tunnel—they added more tunnel! When he flopped out onto that operating table, the doctor took one look at him and said, 'If it doesn't cry in ten seconds, it's a tumor.' Well it only took him two hours to eat his way to the top of the abortion bucket!! He's got a wooden leg—with branches—only it's a wooden leg WITH A REAL FOOT! He's got ten fingers—ALL ON THE SAME HAND! Until one day something caught his eye—AND DRAGGED IT FOR FIFTEEN FEET! Now he's got a glass eye—with a FISH in it! He broke his arm in three places—HE'S NOT GOING BACK TO THOSE PLACES! So he married Lulu the Alligator Girl, who could introduce a lump of coal—into her hole—cross her legs and produce—a DIAMOND IN THE MUFF! Let's have a warm welcome for my hero—the AMAZING MR. LIFTO!!!!"

Tendons stand out like jungle vines on the flushed neck of freak impresario Jim Rose as he hoarsely yells this tale of improbable provenance. Wild-eyed, manic, the master of the modern-day sideshow summons his sidekick Joe Hermann, a.k.a. Mister Lifto, with a flourish. Wearing only shorts and giant blue mountain-climbing carabiners through his pierced ears, Lifto bounces on to the stage, hooks his ears to a bar stool and spins around. The lobes stretch long, absurdly long, as if plied on an old-fashioned taffy machine.

He is a Human Marvel, this man who can also lift seventy pounds with his pierced penis ("that part of him that's most a mister"), 120 pounds with both nipples, and, when the day is done, neatly hang up his clothes on a coat hanger threaded through the central cartilage of his nose. He is an original, one of the founding members of the original Jim Rose Circus that first shocked the world, then inspired a whole generation to experiment with body play, extreme performance and a new concept of sideshow.

And Jim Rose, the sinewy man with the microphone, is the one who first brought together all these strange performers, these disciples of bodily adventure. His troupe of self-made Marvels met in Seattle in 1991. When they joined Perry Farrell's first Lollapalooza show the following year for a cross-country tour, the counterculture was introduced to a sick-out shock-fest the likes of which had never been seen before.

"Thousands of people drank vomit," says Jim Rose proudly. "I would offer it to the audience and they would rush the stage."

The audience also saw sword-swallowing and slug-eating by a curly-haired kid named Paul Lawrence who would later morph himself, through extensive tattooing and surgical procedures, into a living piece of art called The Enigma. Tim Cridland, a.k.a. Zamora the Torture King, performed mystical rites of self-abnegation, shoving giant needles through his face and walking up a ladder of sharpened swords. Bebe the Circus Queen, Jim's French wife, threw pointed darts into her husband's back. And Matt "The Tube" Crowley invented the first gavage act, sucking up a variety of liquids through a tube in his nose and then bringing up the contents of his stomach for an audience refresher.

None of it, save the gavage, was new. All of the acts were once part of the sideshows that operated on fairground midways or in the shadow of traveling circuses. But those sideshows had died out almost exactly a decade earlier, and there was a whole new audience ready for the spectacle of the Jim Rose Circus.

"Jim Rose did a great thing by removing [sideshow] from the traditional context of an amusement park or circus and bringing it to the rock and roll venues—that definitely is Jim's creation," says Dick Zigun, who opened Coney Island's non-profit Sideshows by the Seashore in 1985 to perpetuate the nearly lost American tradition of sideshow.

Canadian sideshow performer Ryan Stock, a regular performer with Jim Rose, puts it this way: "Years ago the sideshow was the side act to the carnival and the circus 'cause that's where the people were, that's where the money was. But today, people go to bars, people go to nightclubs; I think that's where the show should be. The sideshow ends up being the side act to alcohol and dancing, which I don't know if that's a step up or a step down for the sideshow, I guess it's a matter of opinion. The way I look at it, if P.T. Barnum was alive I don't think he'd be herding patrons into a stinky old canvas tent. I think the club owners and the club promoters would become the marks, you know?"

Rock and roll was indeed the hallmark of the Jim Rose Circus, which went on from Lollapalooza to tour the world and perform with a number of groups including Nine Inch Nails and Godsmack. The presentation of the show was entirely fresh: it was scary and funny and moved as fast as a virtuoso guitar riff. The sideshow became a cult phenomenon, with a special episode of the X-Files written for Jim Rose, and The Simpsons treating the performers as cartoon characters. No one had seen anything like it in recent memory, no single sideshow or sideshow performer had been greeted with such adulation in almost a century. And yet...

"Nothing's changed in hundreds of years from the basic formula of getting crowds to react the way you want them to," says Jim, a narrow figure with intense brown eyes. "The only thing I did different was be the first guy not to have a waxy moustache and not to use my diaphragm to do the old—"he puts on a nasal voice—"'All right ladies and gentlemen, step right up, what you're about to see . . .' I just didn't do that. But I'm still using old-school formula. I'm just doing it with a few 'f-' words, in a different voice than yesteryear.

"There's about twenty sideshow stunts that are classics. I like to call them insanity's greatest hits. This is your bed of nails, your bed of blades, your human pincushion, your completely tattooed miscreant, your human dartboard, eating glass. All of that was in my first show. It's all part of this genre to hype, incite and convince people that their lives are incomplete if they don't get in their car, drive to an unfamiliar venue, buy a ticket and watch something their better nature tells them they shouldn't."

A lot of people, thousands, did just that. At Lollapalooza there was something about this tiny side stage full of self-made freaks, proud of their strangeness, a last stand for sheer oddity, that just clicked with young people looking for their own ways of being alternative.

"I think Jim Rose is probably one of the strongest single forces that moved a particular part of our fringe society into the mainstream," says Scott Noe, a friend of Jim Rose and executive producer of his recent travel documentary, the Jim Rose Twisted Tour. "Our culture would be different today without the Jim Rose Circus. I doubt we would see as many tattoos and piercings. It would still be considered fringe and unusual, and today, in 2004, it's mainstream."

Certainly Jim Rose doesn't get all the credit for the changed appearance of America. Perry Farrell and the Lollapalooza show itself were actually responsible for bringing so many together, allowing people to visually sense, for the first time, the full extent of their tribe. Re/Search had recently published "Modern Primitives," a seminal work investigating contemporary experiments with tattoos, piercing and other kinds of body play. So there was a zeitgeist moving among the masses. But the sideshow made it palpable, and the whole notion of sideshow itself became cool again.

"With sideshow entering rock videos and advertising on commercial TV, it's just fully integrated or reintegrated back into American culture. It's probably as influential as it was when there were fifty sideshows touring the country," says Dick Zigun. "When Michael Wilson first worked, aside from being heavily tattooed, he did a shocking act where he hammered a nail through his tongue at every performance. He had a pierced tongue but that wasn't common then. Now every suburban sixteen-year-old girl in America has a pierced tongue and tattoos. And it's partially our bad influence. Really, that's been astonishing to watch, just how influential it's become and knowing how weird and unknown and isolated it was not that long ago."

Jim Rose agrees. "Back when I first started this thing information was obscure and hard to get hold of. There was an underground movement of people who were into this stuff before the Internet made it possible to just click on it. To become a human dartboard I had to watch Third World, grainy footage of an older, retired performer and take some pointers on it."

Jim Rose himself grew up in Phoenix, Arizona, where his first exposure to the carnie life was working at the state fairgrounds. "I'd already been around these Lobster Boys and shit— I had to go fetch 'em fucking Cokes." He studied business in junior college, worked as a car salesman and bug exterminator, and finally met his wife Bebe at a club in D.C. where he was channeling his angst in a spoken word performance. He learned how to eat fire from a street performer, then went to France with Bebe, where he became totally absorbed in the more developed European world of street performing, learning trade secrets and taking notes at every opportunity.

When the optimistic pair returned to the states in 1990, they nearly starved while competing for tips against other performers on Venice Beach in L.A. All day in the sun, on their feet for hours at a time, they attempted to woo the attention of tourists. Jim didn't take too long to develop street smarts and realize that his best act involved his vocal chords. The former car salesman discovered that the trick meant nothing without the pitch, and that he still had a top-notch talent for selling. Soon the crowds were gathering around.

The Enigma recalls his first encounter with Jim in May 1991 at a Seattle street fair. "He was doing that old magic razor blade trick, where you thread the razors on a string inside your mouth. I thought it was really silly because he had this huge crowd of people and he was just doing a magic trick. I swallow swords; that's a real thing. But I didn't know how to be a talker at all. I was young. To be able to speak on stage takes a lot more than just being able to act. You have to be able to talk the talk and walk the walk."

Jim Rose's combustible energy and ability to sell anything, including vomit, to an audience were legendary. His skills made the feats of the Human Marvels seem even more extraordinary. His desire to sell the product was insatiable.

"I was relentless. That's one of the reasons my show was successful," says Jim. "No one would work harder than me. As a matter of fact, every city I went to I told the publicist, 'I dare you to give me more interviews than I can handle. I'll do two at a fucking time. I'll do 'em twenty-four hours straight. I dare you to outwork me. And no one could. I spent two straight years on about four hours sleep a night, relentlessly ensuring that this art form came back in vogue and that my brand name was attached to it so that I could reap some benefits from the work."

The ultimate salesman never really turns off his pitch. Scott Noe recalls the first day of filming a reality series that followed the group—Jim, Bebe, Lifto, Ryan, Cappy the 400-pound yo-yo master, and the Rubber Boy—on a thirty-day trek across the U.S. It was television on the run, with one production crew dashing around filming the freaks every time they stepped off the bus and another crew running around getting release signatures.

"The first place we stop is a Wendy's and they're like 'No, no, turn the cameras off, you can't film in here.' It was a complete meltdown. Jim, who was talent at this point, saw the manager and saw that she was being a complete hard-ass. And Jim grabs the piece of paper from the production assistant and charges up to her and says something that elicits a positive response. As soon as she says yes, he jams the paper in front of her and says, 'Ma'am can you sign this piece of paper?' And she says, 'Is that that location release? I can't sign that.' And he

was like, 'Yes ma'am, it's a location release but I just need you to put your signature on it real quick.' She was like 'I told them I can't sign that.' And he says, "I completely understand that ma'am, and understand why you would have those fears, but let's just get your signature so we can make all of this stop and go away.'

"And I watched him just sit there while she was going 'I'm not doing it, I'm not doing it' and it didn't matter. He wasn't being disrespectful. It was funny; it was hilarious. But to Jim it was a big deal. Did the woman sign the piece of paper? No, she wasn't going to sign it, no one was going to make her sign it. Did that aggravate Jim for at least two to three hours? Absolutely. Did it make a difference at all? No, it was a stupid truck stop. But did it bother Jim because he failed? Yes. He spoke about it and yelled at a few people about how they set it up wrong. It meant the world to Jim and that's what separates Jim Rose from other people. As far as the promotion side of what he does, he really raises that to an art form. Convincing, selling, whatever you call it."

The Jim Rose Circus is credited not only with reviving sideshow to popular consciousness, but with presenting new twists on the genre. "You can't survive off of insanity's greatest hits," Jim says. "Even the sideshows of yesteryear had to continuously evolve. It's coming up with ideas for twenty-first century phobias—things that just didn't come into play during the time when this form of entertainment was prevalent. Like Super Glue. Like power tools. Balancing a running lawn mower on the lip and having audience members throw a head of lettuce at it."

Or like putting your wife in a plastic bag, sucking all the air out with a shrink wrap machine and watching her eyes bug out. Or turning out all the lights and sending masked men running through the audience with loudly buzzing chainsaws. But keeping some old-fash-

ioned goodness in there, as when walking a giant, wiggling scorpion over Bebe the Circus Queen's lovely face.

"I'm no dummy," Jim says. "I know how easy it is to find broken glass and to pound a couple of fucking nails in a board. That's the reason I change too. I knew I was going to get ripped off. That's why you've never seen anyone else bring Mexican transvestite wrestling or women sumo wrestling or a big power tool show. They can't afford to compete, logistically or financially, to do it. That's how you get rid of the competition, you just keep increasing your arms until they can't compete. I learned it from Reagan."

Jim seems unusually preoccupied with the competition generated by his own success, a global success that far outstrips any of the other fringe circuses or sideshows. "It's funny about the imitators," he says. "They all hated me. But the ones that are like twenty-one, twenty-two years old and just starting now—they *love* me! I think the first generation thought they could knock me off the block and were competitive. Everyone's got a 'Look at me! Look at me! Look at me!' situation going, that's why they're in this kind of show. [Performers] quit me. They go out and try to do a show and can't give a ticket away. Every one of them goes out after the show to meet and greet the audience, and eight out of ten people ask them, 'Have you seen the Jim Rose Circus?' It drives them crazy."

It's true that a lot of performers have cycled through the circus over the years—not particularly surprising in show business—and that not a few of them were disgruntled by the experience. Jan T. Gregor, his first tour manager, dished the dirt on Jim's legendary temper in his tell-all narrative *Circus of the Scars: The True Inside Odyssey of a Modern Day Sideshow* (Brennan Dalsgard Publishers, 1998), while many of his current and former employees won't even talk about their association with the sideshow. For those that do, the Lizardman's story is typical.

Erik Sprague, the Lizardman, took over Enigma's slot as the tattooed man in 1999, and rivaled his predecessor with the scope of his body modifications. In addition to wearing a full tattooed bodysuit of lizard-green scales, he also has horn ridge implants above his eyes, teeth filed into sharp points, a split tongue and the word "FREAK" tattooed across his chest. His appearance is so stunning that his photo was once circulated on the floor of the Illinois state legislature during a state representative's unsuccessful attempt to get the procedure of tongue-splitting banned, apparently in fear that all the susceptible teenagers of Illinois would soon be resembling reptiles.

"I don't like Jim's personality type. I never had a good time," says the Lizardman. "It wasn't horrible, but by the same token no matter how good things were there was always a down side. It was that guy over there. Literally now I don't speak his name as a general rule.

"Rikki Lake wanted me to be on the show in 1999 and the first time that they tried to set it up they went through him. And he got mad at the production assistant—he bitched her out because he wanted to make sure his name was on the screen every time I was on camera. Once he swore at her she hung up the phone. He was blacklisted off the show and me along with him. Luckily I was able to set it up later and it worked out beautifully. That is very indicative of my experience and how my life was messed up being around him."

"Owning a circus is like pushing a wheelbarrow full of bullfrogs," says Jim. "We're not the fucking Beatles. We don't step into a room together and write 'I Wanna Hold Your Hand.' Everybody has their turn on stage and does something. They're competing with each other. Unfortunately my position in this profession makes people hate me. If you need attention and you're not getting as much as you think you need and you're not able to blame it on yourself, you're going to put the blame somewhere else."

"The one part of my job I never liked was being a boss in such close quarters," he continues. "A bus is a psychological test tube on wheels. You can't get away from people in ways you would like to sometimes. And the very nature of the people I tour with—they're in a freakshow for godssakes. They're doing things their mothers told them *not to do*. Hell, I catch myself trying to talk 'em out of doing stuff. I'm 47-years old now—older than some of these guys' fathers."

The circus has toned down some of its grotesqueries and actually plays to a theater crowd when abroad. The droves of people who used to faint during a show are much fewer. "We're actually considered legitimate theater," says Jim. "And we do a much better show when we're in a theater, too. You don't have to scream and yell and keep the energy so high. You can actually talk to [the audience] and be a little clever and it works.

"It's really about the power of presentation. I could get a lot of people to faint doing the human dartboard, presenting it differently. In 1994 I presented a lot of the same acts with more comedy than maniacal depravity, and I started noticing there were less falling ovations.

This was just before Jerry Springer quit acting like Oprah—we had a real sea change once that happened. When Jerry Springer realized he couldn't make highbrow he went to the gutter. Which is where a sideshow is. From that point on, people got a bit desensitized. But right before that sea change I had changed my presentation and was getting *out* of the gutter while everyone else was going *to* the gutter. Which is basically my m.o. I'm a contrarian. And a decent train spotter."

The Jim Rose Circus may have seen its glory days. At the moment, the troupe only convenes for special occasions, and Jim Rose himself is living in Las Vegas, playing poker.

"Frankly I don't need to work anymore," he says. "If some hotshot kid came along and decided to put together something completely new and innovative together—if he's not trashing me—I'd probably support him. I'd love to find someone who can come up with a creative idea on their own, not just a rehashing of the same old stunts, so that it does continue after the Jim Rose Circus. Because I did what I set out to do. Now I'm just going around, reveling and having fun with my fans. I don't really have anything left to prove."

10
END★
OF
THE
WORLD
CIRKUS★
&
KNOW
NOTHING
ZIRKUS
&ZIDESHOW★

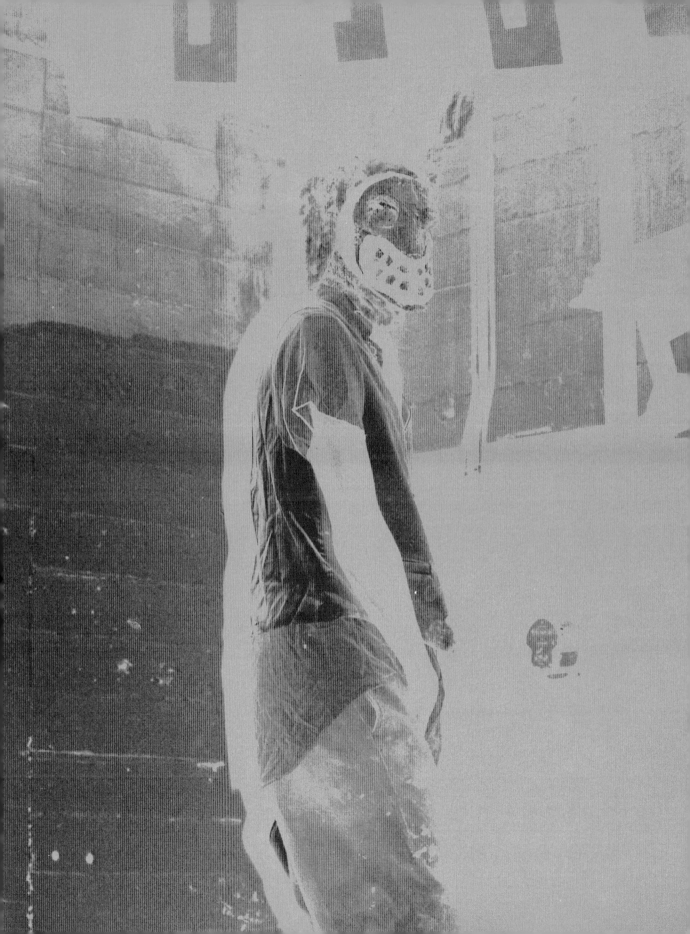

A UNICYCLE WITH flaming pedals zooms into the audience, sending spectators scattering across the warehouse floor. Fred Normal, the cyclist, a curved horn sitting on top of his head like a demented party favor, makes a few more passes through the skittish crowd. He hops off his bike and hoists it overhead, throws his head back and extinguishes the pedals by lowering each one into his mouth.

It's a penultimate display of fire eating, but the other performers are not easily outdone. Camanda Galactica—early in her quest to become the World's Only Circus Gypsy Superhero Sideshow Cabaret Starlet—drops into the splits on the concrete floor while sinuously waving finger extensions tipped with fire. Her long hair is matted into snaky brown dreads, armpit hair peeking over the top of her red vinyl bra, long legs and untrimmed pubic hair jutting out of her stripper's G-string. She jumps up and runs over to play the drums, where two others are already pounding on what looks like an anarchic jumble of three drum kits.

There's not really a stage, per se, just an area where the musicians have consolidated their gear. Chaos is happening everywhere. A monster puppet head waves over the crowd. About six girls dressed as cheerleaders appear and began leading a cheer: "Shoot—the rapist! Shoot, shoot the rapist!" A feminist statement, perhaps? A styrofoam head and a styrofoam sea horse dance together. A naked man walks around with a red rubber ball strapped to his forehead. Over the drum noise, a girl wearing nothing but pink panties plays slide trombone, somewhere on the borderline between improvised jazz and sheer noise. She straddles a sawhorse, plays upside down for awhile, then places the fluted opening of her trombone over a guy's crotch, giving him a brief musical blowjob. A giant, skeletal puppet manned by three people stalks through the warehouse with flaming hands and a shrouded head. There are hula-hoops, odd characters in green metallic capes, random pie-throwing and a dog wandering through the whole performance, wagging its tail.

"That's what the End of the World was really like—people can't believe what they were seeing was entertainment," says circus co-founder Ed the Clown. "That was actually the thought: If the world was to come to an end and there were no more entertainment sources—TV or radio—if there was nothing else, if the world was over, if Y2K happened, *this* is what you would get for entertainment. People subtly got it and they loved it. They were like 'Wow, you guys are really trying.' We were."

The scenes taken from a handheld video camera are date-stamped May 30, 1999. It's a significant date. In just a few days the End of the World Cirkus, a disorganized group of unwashed, tattooed, dumpster-diving vagabonds, was fated to meet the Know Nothing Family Zirkus/Zideshow, a copycat group of freaks with the most profane, bodily fluid-soaked show ever to escape the notice of local law enforcement. Together they would create a traveling apocalypse that lured dozens of would-be performers onto the caravan, only to see them fall off when they became too tired, hungry, disillusioned or simply distracted to continue. For most participants it was equally the best of times and the worst of times. Lives would be saved and limbs would be lost. And the definition of circus, to a certain segment of society, would forever be changed.

The revolution began with puppets.

Ed had developed a shadow puppet show that he called The Circus of Tiny Invisibility to perform alongside Copro Lingus, a band that in turn was touring as part of the Nomadic Festival in 1996. The puppet show featured the antics of a group of aliens called the Tiny Invisibles who were responsible for all sorts of mayhem, both within the puppet show and outside, amidst the festival at large. Camanda, Ed's girlfriend, stood in front of the screen and served as ringmistress over the Tiny Invisibles.

The Nomads, formed by a group of squatters and anarchists on New York's Lower East Side, had begun traveling the previous year, putting on circus-like shows and workshops urging people to free themselves from the norms of capitalist society. Essentially, these street punks had figured out that "performing" was a better way to make a living than actual begging. Both took place on the street, but one was a lot more fun than the other.

Ed, Camanda and three other friends all piled into a station wagon in Texas in the summer of 1996 to hook up with Copro Lingus at Burning Man. Once in the desert, they met a daredevil named Fredrick Ulysses Normal (F.U.N.) and many other of the original circus kids that formed End of the World: Mary-Go-Round, Joe Mama, Pierre Pressure, John Joyce. The Bindlestiff Family Cirkus was also there.

"The first time I ever saw them Stephanie was screaming on top of this big—it wasn't even a stage—it was more like boxes and a truck," recalls Ed. "It was a big huge show but they were all wearing the same dirty clothes, they weren't in costumes or anything. She was up there screaming 'This is what we do for a living!' And I was like, 'Whoa, you can do this for a *living?*' I can honestly say it was the Bindlestiffs that turned me into a circus kid. I think I kind of had it in me already, I just didn't know what to call it."

"From then on my friends and I started living the circus tradition lifestyle. We're not pretending to be in the circus, we're *in* the circus because we live the life that circus people had to live. We're pulling up, we're doing a show, we're leaving, we're getting someplace, we're meeting people. When thirty people band together and identify with the traditions it's best to call it circus."

The Circus of Tiny Invisibility attracted more puppeteers and pranksters as it continued traveling with the Nomadic Festival. In 1998, with the millennium approaching, the Nomads called their tour the "End of the World" tour, but by the end of the year, the Circus of Tiny Invisibility and a number of other performers were just calling themselves the End of the World Cirkus. "The Nomadic Festival was married to the idea of doing workshops," remembers Camanda, "and we wanted the freedom to perform in different venues."

The End of the World was something. It pulled into towns unannounced with ten vehicles (including a converted school bus), a tangle of mutant bicycles, three or four dogs, and thirty-plus people—half of them drunk and sleeping, and the other half trying to get a show started. There were never any pre-booked engagements, just some phone calls made to friends on arrival. The circus family lived on incredibly intimate terms: sleeping together, eating meals together and, mostly, playing together.

"We get into town and we just try to find someone who's willing to put us up," says Ed. "And then their house is totally mobbed by this big huge rambling group of freaks. [On] show day everyone is scrambling to dress themselves and to eat and to get high, and everybody's in a constant frenzy over how this thing is gonna work. The core of us would put together a set list. That's where I actually had a job; I had to ask everybody what they were gonna do. And I would put it on a list and then I'd take it back and we'd try to figure out the best order to put it in. And once the set list was out, then everybody started panicking; they were like, 'Where am I? When am I next? Who am I after?' And then for about two hours nobody really had a clue what was happening."

The result was a disorienting explosion of freak exhibitionism. The show included Mary Go-Round and her flaming hula hoops, Dr. Otis performing shadow "clown surgery" on an audience member from behind a backlit scrim, Ed playing xylophone with whips, a giant puppet snake, DJs and fire performers. There was machete juggling, bike jousting, a Human Cannonball act and the Ramp of Death.

"We had a little ramp, really small, and we set it down and someone on a bike tries jumping over it. There's a lot of variations but essentially someone tries to jump it and can't seem to do it," says Ed. "Eventually we pour gasoline over the whole board and light it on fire and people go crazy, we get everyone chanting 'Ramp of Death!' and whoever's doing it goes over the ramp. By the end of it the audience is ready for blood or something."

The End of the World performed in Pierre Pressure's hometown of Cherrymont, Pa., where they did a show for his grandmother and other assorted guests. "We did the Ramp of Death and got everybody chanting," recalls Ed. "And then down towards the end of the show we're like, 'Okay, we're gonna take a request from Granny—what does Granny want to see? She's like ninety years old, and she just stood up and started yelling 'Ramp of Death!' Everybody just fell to the ground [laughing] and then started chanting with her, about a hundred people. And we're like, 'She wants it, here it comes!'"

Another classic circus entertainment was "What's Up Your Ass?", an interactive game pioneered a few years earlier by Cirkus Redickuless. In this segment, audience members were invited to get on stage, drop their pants, and let circus kids place objects between their butt cheeks. "We put tape balls, vibrating hamsters, plungers, knives, Barbie dolls, whatever we could find," says Ed. And the grand finale: fireworks.

"We were laughing so hard because it was always unbelievable that people would let us bring 'em up onstage, put stuff in their butts and usually at the end light fireworks out of someone's butt. We always picked someone impactful for that, somebody that everyone at the establishment might know. You get the right target and man, putting firecrackers in somebody's butt that everyone looks up to is hilarious. It's like this big huge release. They're like, 'That's our boss with firecrackers up his ass.'"

The last act, Betty Cannonball, was representative of the whole circus. The human cannonball act would be built up throughout the show, and when black-haired Betty Cannonball came running out with goggles, kneepads and a lightening bolt painted on her shirtfront, the audience really thought it was going to see something. What they saw was Betty, balanced on a teeterboard inside a cardboard tube, pop out the other end of the tube when Ed jumped on the teeterboard. But she'd run around the room with such drama and flair that the audience fell for it anyway and gave up enthusiastic applause. It was more fun to join the inanity than to grumble about being duped.

Although the End of the World got pretty wild when performing for their own kind, they did a lot of family-friendly shows as well, even performing at Martha's Vineyard during the high tourist season. They easily switched gears from crass to simply stupid. "The circus had a good child-like quality," says Ed. "It was genuine fun."

Enter the Know Nothings.

The Know Nothing Family Zirkus/ Zideshow was represented by Dr. Eric Von Know Nothing, a skinny kid with bright red dyed hair sticking straight up from his scalp à la Johnny Rotten. Ambition lurked behind his light blue eyes and youthful appearance. He was the talker of the show, the one whose job was to introduce . . .

Flag Blash-Point, the rubber man who could suck his own cock on a bed of nails,

Micki Luv, a rock star fire performer who could illuminate a lightbulb placed in her vagina,

Stix the Clown, who put a running elec-tric drill up his urethra,

Aura Fist, a female Lifto, who hoisted a six-pack of beer from her labia piercings, then invited audience members to drink the dangling refreshments,

Nostril Dumb-Ass, who gave himself an enema onstage and drank his own brew,

and Ludwig, a.k.a. Piss Puddles the Clown, who made beautiful, amazing, gigantic puppets.

They called their show "the greatest evening you will ever spend in Hell."

The Know Nothings had been festering down in New Orleans where they had taken over an open mike night at a club in the ninth ward called the Hi-Ho Lounge, a dive with beat-up couches that sold cheap drinks and ramen noodles. The Hi-Ho's "Not So Ladylike Ladies' Night" on Wednesdays featured the earliest sideshow members and their friends, people like Satan John, a local character with semi-permanent fangs who could put out a flaming match placed over a woman's bare nipple with a single flick from one of his handmade whips.

The End of the World wound up its '98 tour at the Autonomous Mutant Festival in Portland, Oregon, where they encountered the Know Nothings, who were walking around with shaved heads and sporting a "We have lice" sign at their camp. The End of the World crew thought that the Know Nothings were hysterically funny. They did a show together, in the woods. Flag Blash-Point, unannounced and completely stoned, premiered his bed of nails, did a nude yoga plow pose on the sharpened tips, dropped his knees behind his shoulders and his penis into his mouth. The crowd went wild and the End of the World master of ceremonies, according to Flag's memory, "totally lost his shit. It made them really think about the Know Nothings."

It was agreed that the following year, when the circus came through New Orleans, the Know Nothings would join the tour.

The circus had officially gained its own sideshow, a time-honored partnership. At their first show together, the Know

Nothings wowed the End of the World by debuting the puppet rock opera "Rock-A-Zulu," with a proliferation of giant, crazy-looking puppets courtesy of Ludwig. But the Know Nothings had more than puppets up their sleeve. Many of the End of the World crew were quickly appalled.

"Ludwig was a genius creator, a genius artist, and you know what they had him doing in their show?" asks Ed. "Gargle pee. Can you believe that?"

A Know Nothing scenario would call for Ludwig to be "punished" and Amy ("All-Day Ass"), wearing a giant Vagina Monster puppet/costume with a hole in it, would pee into his mouth. Then Eric would take musical requests from the audience and put the microphone up to Ludwig's mouth.

"This guy is phenomenal, he's one of the most amazing artists we know. And the Know Nothings?" Ed, still outraged, switches to a low, shifty voice. "'Uh, Lud—can you do that gargling pee thing again? Can you gargle 'Iron Man'?'" He returns to his normal voice. "The Know Nothings, man. They underutilized a lot of the great talent they had. They were being exploited by Eric and his perception of performing."

In a way, though, the two groups were meant for each other. *Eschatology*, the study of last things, is also closely related to the Greek word *skato-*, from which is derived scat or shit. The End of the World, an exploration into the final forms of entertainment at the end of civilization, was bound to result in the waste & orifice-obsessed Know Nothings.

Puppets never disappeared entirely from the Know Nothings' repertoire, but after the first performance the group quickly determined what kind of gut-wrenching, hardcore, sideshow-for-the-new-millennium they wanted to be. Artistic differences created tension between the two groups from the beginning; soon enough they began squabbling over money as well.

"We were forced to make our own money on the 2000 tour," says Eric. "The End of the World wasn't sharing with us and they kept trying to absorb our show even though they didn't like what we did. We kept having these big meetings with everybody yelling at us, and me smiling and nodding...

"So what we would do is build up our own show all through the End of the World, and by the end people would want to see it because their show sucked so bad. They weren't giving us gas money or anything, they were trying to make us fall off the tour, so that was our reaction. We'll survive any way we can. While End of the World was doing their show we'd find an area nearby, or in back of the club, and charge people to come in afterwards, between one and five [A.M.]."

As the two groups traveled together their ranks were swelled by all sorts of itinerate, unemployed, or idealistic young would-be gypsies. They were attracted by a lifestyle that suggested there didn't have to be a distinction between the outside world and circus life, between performing and simply being. They would simply create their own environment wherever they went by the sheer magnitude of their props, crazy bikes and colorful clothes. Gutter punks and grad school dropouts hopped aboard the circus wagon, which by then was holding about fifty people. Often it was unclear what these newer arrivals contributed to the show other than the already-established chaos.

"The End of the World had this habit of picking up anybody and everybody that could come up with an act," says Eric. "But since they had this *attitude* about doing children's entertainment, they didn't want to sully their name and wouldn't let people do things. So we ended up taking their rejects. That's how we ended up with Nostril."

Nostril Dumb-Ass is the stuff of legend. Nostril's main act would be to give himself an enema with a turkey baster filled with wine or water, and then drink his own, liquefied shit. His costume was a diaper and a dunce cap, accessorized with two puppet hands that looked like giant hypodermic needles.

"Nostril was an extreme example of circus at its ugliest," says Josh Simmons, a.k.a. Spanky Ass-Blood the Clown, an early member of the Know Nothings. "I don't think there was anything that crossed my boundary except watching Nostril eat his own shit. Actually I was okay with that. But for some reason when Pierre Pressure would puke in Nostril's mouth, that kind of almost made me gag. Because Pierre can puke on command. Nostril would be down on his knees and Pierre would be towering over him and then Pierre would just vomit in his mouth."

"Nostril's had a lot of problems in his life and now he has more," adds Eric. "That year Pierre tattooed clown makeup on Nostril's face, which started off okay, he looked classy. But later on in his career Nostril wound up getting some extra tattoos, at first little decorations on the clown makeup. Later he winds up getting a John Waters moustache and "INNER CONFLICT" tattooed across his forehead. Now he's just a total mess."

Nostril wasn't the only one with issues.

"My circus friends are all abusive, or were abusive to some degree, self-abusive that is," says Ed. "Most of the people who were in it were saved from their own addiction or saved from bad environments. For a lot of us [circus] was a way to focus and get away from a lot of bullshit."

Some people may have found a way out of their addictions; others unquestionably seized the opportunity to indulge them. And yet there was an overarching nobility to the group's mission, which carried on the Nomadic Festival tradition of planting seeds of subversion, of resistance to a life of mere passive acquisition. "We traveled to all these weird places where they just don't have exposure to this kind of life," says Camanda. "At first, when they see this band of smelly weird-looking freaks with dreadlocked hair their first reaction is to call the cops. Then you start juggling and entertaining the . . . and they'll have a conversation with you. They realize you're not so weird, you're a normal person, you watch the same movies . . .

"It causes people to question 'What am I doing with my life?' Sometimes you get people saying "'I can never do what you guys do, I just can't run away.' All defensive. And I'm like, 'I'm not telling you to run away and do this, 'cause if you did I wouldn't have a job. It's metaphorical—run away and join whatever it is that makes *you* happy.' It was so cool to come back through the next year and see how many people had quit their jobs and were doing other things. That was my driving force for sure."

Inspiration was needed to keep the group going. Food, money and gas were scarce; the performers had to be resourceful to avoid literally becoming starving artists. It got tough at times.

"You'd get a cup of coffee to get you through the day; for me coffee shrinks your stomach so you don't have to eat so much," remembers Josh, a cartoonist who chronicled some of the circus' adventures in a comic book series.

"We were dumpstering. I remember one of the first shows in Pensacola, Florida, me and Forest [a former drummer for Crash Worship] went behind a grocery store and found twenty cakes and pies. So we'd get stuff like that. Forest is an amazing dumpster diver who always find things for people to eat and get by. And certain folks like Amy [All-Day Ass] and Camanda were like moms of the group, where they'd end up taking on a disproportionate amount of the struggle to get food. With fifty people there was a lot of dead weight, people who didn't have a real act or contribute much in the way of money, food or a ride."

"It became really frustrating," says Camanda. "We got harsh as far as asking people 'What is your act? What do you do?' and trying to make some sort of system with which people got the money . . . and not everybody was happy. Survival was the key. I got really protective, which helped increase my reputation as a raging bitch. I didn't have time to hold people's hands and say 'Would you please wash your dishes?' My first approach to anyone who wanted to come in was like, 'Who the hell are you and what do you want with my people?' We were

working really hard for whatever it was we were doing, to get eight vehicles across the country and all those people to make it to the end. That was the goal—could we fucking do it?"

In New Orleans, the Know Nothing's hometown, Nostril invited two new friends to join the circus. Both were gutter punks who had spent time doing some protest tree-sitting in California.

"Stix turned out to be one of the funniest clowns we've ever met; he's a really funny guy and he slowly developed into being a clown," says Ed. "But Dan didn't."

The story of Dan is retold like a Biblical account of the gods' retribution for the sin of being dead weight.

"Dan was always drinking all our beer," Ed continues. "He'd go to the shows and get drunk and he wouldn't do anything, he'd just lie there. It drove everybody nuts. He'd be eating the food that people were cooking for us. And then he'd always be grumbling. We said, 'You know, you've really got to get an act.' He'd pretend to try but then he really couldn't. He never found anything to do."

The circus hauled Dan all the way from New Orleans to Columbus, Ohio, urging him all the way to get an act. "While we were in Columbus he was riding around on a tall bike—you know, two on top of each other—so he's riding around on a tall bike, basically wasting time, and he goes around a corner and he doesn't see an awning coming off a building, and so he *gouges* out his eye. And *thunk*, that puts him on the ground and there's blood everywhere and his right eye is gouged out and he's in the hospital. And everyone is like, 'Oh my god, what has happened to Dan?' His parents find out and they send him some new clothes and every-thing, and tell him that they're coming to get him. We're like 'Whoa, this is really funny. People run away *to* the circus, they never run away *from* it.' And three days later here his parents are taking him away."

Dan didn't want to go, but the circus members, wearing the clean socks and T-shirts that had arrived in his parents' care package, cheerily waved good-bye.

"But the story continues," says Ed. "When we reach the west coast, he skips out on his parents in Kansas City and joins the circus again. And while he's at Autonomous Mutant Fest, he's riding around on a tall bike. And because he can't see, his vision hasn't adjusted, he falls off a bridge and he rolls down this ravine and gets all cut up. No one can believe it, they're like, 'What is up with this man? He's obviously asking for it.'

"So the summer continues and everyone's out at Burning Man now, and at Burning Man we're asking him, 'Hey now, what do you do? What's your act?' We're all trying to figure out a trick he can do with his one eye. And here he is, doing what? Drinking our beer, eating our food . . . . People are saying, 'Man, you've gotta do something about that—find yourself an act.' Here's the beauty part of it: at the end of Burning Man he decides to hop a train. Him and his friends get together and they're taking off out of Nevada, and they're going to hop a train but he hasn't learned to adjust his vision yet. So he goes for the train and he misses it and both his legs are cut off. I'm not kidding.

"No one believes it until someone gets back to Kansas City and the story is confirmed, months and months later. That Mardi Gras [in New Orleans] he comes up to us in a wheel-chair and the first thing he says is, 'Hey look, Ed, I got an act.' And we all just busted out laughing. He's going around telling people, 'Hey you might remember me, I used to be taller.' We were like 'Whoa—you've got an act *and you're funny*.' Now he's special to us.

"It's a harsh story but that's the reality. God gave him ample opportunity—three months, four months. His parents tried to save him. He didn't listen. But he is much funnier now and he's a much better person. Circus saves lives. It also tore some up but the lifesaving thing—Dan is a good example. He learned a valuable lesson, and he's okay with it. He's got no choice. With most of us that's how it is."

Something strange and unforeseeable happened after the first year of touring together: the Know Nothings, that rag-tag bunch of gross-out artists, started to get really good. Their show took place in a specific chronological order, rather than amidst the mass chaos favored by End of the World. Their timing got tighter and they added more comedy and staging techniques to complement the vile spectacle of bodily effluent. All this improvement, however, didn't prevent them from getting banned from their favorite club in New Orleans, the Howling Wolf, where Eric did his version of William Tell.

Eric's act involved his girlfriend Micki, an apple and a 9 mm handgun. Stix the Clown would stand behind Micki with a board to catch the bullet after it went through the apple. After Eric made his shot and got a round of applause, Stix looked down and appeared to notice for the first time an empty hole in the board. He started shaking and yelling for an ambulance, and eventually spit up a mouthful of blood and a 9 mm shell. It was a good act—and one that freaked out a number of club owners. The manager of the Howling Wolf asked them not to return.

Ed the Clown noticed that the Know Nothings were getting better, but he and his friends weren't moved to emulate them. "A lot of things made End of the World great – it's spontaneity, it's unrehearsed nature, the feeling like it's running out of control," he said. "The Know Nothings' problem was that within a year they got really polished to the point that their show was essentially the same show every time. That's not fun. Sure, the other people in the next town haven't seen it but you're not creating energy for yourself. You're not creating the excitement for yourself, so big deal if you do a really tight show."

"Eric wanted to turn it into a real circus and he started telling people what to do," says John Husted, a.k.a. Satan John. That didn't sit well with the extremely freaky people who had escaped the bounds of conventional society to join a hardcore, chaotic sideshow. "Eric's desire to control and his ego drove people away."

By the 2001 tour, the Know Nothings were down to thirteen performers, while the End of the World was losing membership as well. A few of the End of the World people thought that Eric had the right idea; Camanda, who had taken the initiative earlier to do advance booking for End of the World, started booking for the Know Nothings instead. Competition between the two groups grew even more heated. A number of people decided that with all the group politics, the circus was in fact no longer fun—the kiss of death for an underground circus. If living like a gypsy, eating out of dumpsters, and juggling for gas money to the next town wasn't fun, then what was the point?

The next year was the end of the road for both the End of the World and the Know Nothings. The Know Nothings went out on their own, retracing the path of the previous year up the east coast and then west to California.

They had dropped the most disgusting acts in the show involving body fluids, mainly because the people willing to perform them were no longer there. The Know Nothings were down to just four—Eric, Micki, Flag and Juan—but they had the sideshow down to its tightest rendition ever, reserving just two of their sexually-oriented stunts for the very end.

Micki did electricity stunts throughout the show, placing a 9-volt battery on her tongue and then lighting torches off her skin or shocking audience members. For the grand finale, Juan, the lighting tech, would flood the whole stage with angelic blue lighting. Micki, center stage, would do a headstand, place the battery on her tongue and then spread her legs. A light-bulb was placed in her vagina. Eric and Flag were standing to one side.

"We would all put on sunglasses and stand like we were in church," says Eric. "Then the lightbulb lights up, it was kind of this 'it's a miracle' thing, but we're dead serious. There were many times when we could get the whole audience to start screaming, 'We believe!'"

Then a cacophony of noise and a red light washed the stage while Flag did contortions on the bed of nails, ending with an autofellating pose.

"People wouldn't know what to believe because it was so dead-set dramatic and serious, but it was totally tongue-in-cheek the whole time," says Eric. "We had so few people that if anyone dropped the ball that whole momentum crashed. We really bombed in San Francisco because

of that and because the audience was really tough; they weren't willing to go along with us. But when it worked it was beautiful."

Ed followed the Know Nothings around the country, nipping at their heels with the remains of End of the World. They were down to a few puppeteers, two jugglers and an accordion player. It resembled the original kernel of a whimsical, shabby show that had later blossomed so extravagantly, if temporarily, into a freak liberation movement.

"That's what we did before—we tricked people into believing they were entertained, and from there they went on to entertain themselves," says Ed. "One of the mantras we used to have was, 'We're not exploiting people, we're teaching people how to exploit themselves.' That's what we're still doing. Everyone's learning how to do it."

Acknowledgements

Heartfelt thanks to Jeff Barfoot and Casey McGarr for their original artwork, Ellen Daniels for initial encouragement and editing, Caron Hill for the loan of frequent flyer miles, and Ammi Emergency of Soft Skull Press for her enthusiasm and steely determination to see this project through to the finish. A special thanks to those groups who shared their time and stories, but unfortunately were not included in the final version of the book: The Blue Monkey Sideshow, Circus Amok, Cirque de Flambé and Ignis Devoco.

Circus Contraption	Phil Hollenbeck
Zamora	Phil Hollenbeck
Flam Chen	Phil Hollenbeck
Enigma	Phil Hollenbeck
Cloudseeding	p. 73: Phil Hollenbeck
	p. 78: Tom Richardson (bunny w/pork chop)
	p. 79: Kelie Bowman
	pp. 81–82: Tom Richardson
	p. 86: Phil Hollenbeck
Bantu	p. 91–99: Phil Hollenbeck
	pp. 100–104: J. Dee Hill
Yard Dogs	Phil Hollenbeck
Bindlestiffs	Phil Hollenbeck
Jim Rose	Color photo by Mark van S.
	Others by Jan T. Gregor
End of the World	p. 159: Josh Simmons
	p. 162 top: Elana Koff; bottom: Josh Simmons
	p. 165: Josh Simmons
	pp.166–167: Shannon Brinkman
	p. 168 top, mid: Josh Simmons; bottom: Elana Koff
	p. 171: Elana Koff
	p. 172: Shannon Brinkman
	p. 175: Josh Simmons